Children who care

**Inside the World of
Young Carers**

Jo Aldridge and Saul Becker

Jo Aldridge is a Research Officer in the
Department of Social Sciences, Loughborough
University and a former international
journalist.

Dr Saul Becker is Director of Studies for the
interdisciplinary Masters Degree programme
in Policy, Organisation and Change in
Professional Care, Department of Social
Sciences, Loughborough University.

 Loughborough
University

Loughborough University
Department of Social Sciences

First published 1993 by
DEPARTMENT OF SOCIAL SCIENCES
Loughborough University, Leicestershire
LE11 3TU
Published in association with
Nottinghamshire Association of Voluntary
Organisations
1 Byron Street, Mansfield, Nottinghamshire
NG18 5NX

Designed by Justin Costley
Typeset in 10/15 pt. Palatino.
Printed and bound in Great Britain by
Billingham Press Ltd
Front cover designed and illustrated by Eco
Consulting

British Library Cataloguing-in-Publication
Data.
A catalogue record for this book is available
from the British Library

ISBN 0 907274 01 3

Contents

List of Tables and Boxes

Acknowledgements

This research was funded by Joint Finance through Nottinghamshire Association of Voluntary Organisations (NAVO) and our grateful thanks are extended to the above and in particular to Jon North, NAVO Co-ordinator. Further thanks are extended to the following members of the Young Carers Project Steering group, for their continued advice and support throughout the project's duration:

Wendy Adcock, Kathleen Archer, Sandra Bannerman, Susie Daniel, Ann Fletcher, Al Kestenbaum, Celia Knight, Janice Knight, Caroline Marshall, Jon North, Leon Polnay, Jane Sterck, Maeve Stinson, Pam Wisher.

We acknowledge the initial support of the Carers National Association Young Carers Project Co-ordinator, Huw Meredith and later his successor Sylvia Heal.

Our grateful thanks are extended to Kay Aldridge for transcribing the taped interviews, and of course to the young carers and their families without whose co-operation and patience this research would not have been possible.

Foreword

When I think about all those years I cared for my dad, it makes me angry, not because I had to care for him - I *wanted* to care for him - but because I was left alone to cope with his illness for so long.

I wasn't just doing ordinary tasks like other kids might do around the house. I was having to cook for him, beg for money and food parcels so I could feed him, take him to the toilet, clean him up when he couldn't get to the toilet - because he couldn't get up the stairs towards the end.

No one should have to see their parents like that, when they lose all their bodily functions. I loved my dad and I couldn't bear to see him losing his dignity - getting more ill before my eyes. But because I loved him, I wanted to be with him. I wanted to look after him. I just wish someone could have helped me and that those who interfered in our lives and made them difficult could have left us alone.

All I ever wanted was to talk to someone and someone who could have warned me about my dad's fits, caused by his brain tumour.

It's too late for me now. My dad died and I'm no longer a 'young carer', but for all those other kids out there who are in the same situation I was, then something should be done to help them. Not take them away from their mum or dad, but to help them care without worrying, without being frightened.

Jimmy
(16 years)

Introduction

There are no precise figures as to the number of young carers in Nottingham or Nottinghamshire. However, we are able to extrapolate from other studies conducted in Tameside and Sandwell (O'Neill, 1988; Page, 1988) which indicate a national figure of 10,000 children who care. Locally, in Nottinghamshire, this suggests a figure of at least 300 young carers with *primary* caring responsibilities. There will be many more children who *share* the care with others.

The numbers may not be large, but as we reveal in this study, the impact of caring in relation to a child's development and opportunities, can be profound.

For the sake of brevity, we refer in this report to 'young carers', by which we mean those people under the age of 18 who are providing primary care for a sick or disabled relative in the home. However, we have called this report and dedicated the findings to '*children* who care'. In referring to these children we wish to draw attention to their status in society; that in relation to public and professional judgements and pronouncements, they are often powerless and, despite their considerable responsibilities as carers, are always regarded as subordinate to adults. As carers they may have revealed their competence and maturity through the provision and management of care, but in reality they are still children - with few rights and little authority. The experiences and specific needs of children who care have been largely ignored.

It is important to recognise distinctions within 'informal' (unpaid) caring and to avoid regarding carers as a homogeneous group. The age distinction is an important one, as a young carer's status as a child means she or he has particular needs which are age and developmentally specific. If we are to provide for these needs effectively it is imperative that we determine what the reality and experience of young caring is, and, through direct communication with children who care, make suggestions and recommendations for their welfare, on the basis of *their* expressed needs.

Moreover, we have to look at the dilemma, contradictions and tensions in young caring between the traditional role of a child who needs love, support and to be taken care of (ie responsibility for the child's well being lies with the parent, guardian or substitute family) and the role of the young carer where the child *is* the guardian of their own parent's welfare. We have to examine the effects of caring on a child's educational and psycho-social development.

It is also important to try and reconcile the dilemma between the liberation and protection argument - whether to intervene in children's lives to protect them from harm or too much responsibility, or to liberate them by empowering them and promoting their financial and emotional independence. Only through listening to young carers and observing their experiences and expressed needs do we go some way to resolving this dilemma.

Furthermore, with the implementation of the Children Act and the NHS and Community Care Act, it is important that we highlight the needs of young carers and that they are included in new service arrangements. The foundations are laid for their inclusion in policy. For example the legislation requires local authorities to listen and observe the views and experiences of carers - young carers must also be included in this. The Children Act defines and clarifies the rights of children - and implies a notion of childhood that is safe and protected. It also prioritises options which endeavour to keep children in the family whenever possible and local authorities must provide services where children's welfare is at stake - these requirements must be informed and supported by the evidence and statements of young carers in the community.

However, despite these national developments, there is evidence that at a local level carers' needs are 'slipping away from centre stage' (Hadley, 1992:1). If this is true in relation to carers generally, what chance do young carers have for recognition and support?

We hope that this research will help to put the needs of children who care onto the community care, child care and policy agenda. Through the individual accounts which unfold in the following chapters, one story emerges about the day to day lives of young carers - their stresses, their fears and their needs.

We do not believe that these accounts are any more or less shocking than other young carers' stories. They have not been selected because of the severity of their circumstances and experiences. The young carers in our study were chosen simply because of their accessibility. In some cases it was not *that* easy to find them, but access was aided by the multi-disciplinary steering group who supported the research. There might be an argument to suggest that those young carers who aren't accessible - who remain even more hidden - may have even more exceptional accounts to give.

The Literature Reviewed 1

Introduction

Considering the recent awareness of the issue of young caring, it is perhaps not surprising that the literature review did not uncover a substantial body of work on the subject. Indeed, just as attention in terms of policy making and service provision has traditionally focused on the conditions and needs of the care receiver (or service 'user' as they are often termed), then so too has the literature. Although more recently attention has focused on the circumstances and needs of informal carers, there is a dearth of literature on *young* carers, as we define them as those children under the age of 18 who are providing primary care for a sick or disabled relative in the home. They are excluded from the arena of community care debate, just as they are from the attention of service providers.

The hidden world of young carers may partly be a product of definition. Although there have been one or two small scale studies providing general statistical data on young carers, other literature *has* included reference to the young caring experience without actually defining young carers as an autonomous group. Thus, they are presented as an adjunct to a different, adult subject group. For example, the cared-for person or service user. The very words 'service user' to denote the primary subject also imply that the young carers *of* the service user are not service users - or may not need services - themselves.

Despite recent awareness of the issue, it seems that child carers have existed for centuries. There is considerable evidence that the reality of children caring for a sick or disabled relative in the home can be historically attested, but that, as is the case until quite recently, their presence has gone largely unrecognised and their experiences, characteristics, needs and contribution have gone largely undocumented.

A Historical Perspective - Images and Evidence of Young Carers

Images of young carers can be traced throughout history. Novellic images can be cited, for example in the works of Dickens and Hardy. In Dickens' *Little Dorrit* (1857) the character takes on the role of 'little mother' (Chapter 9) and takes responsibility for her family at a very early age. By the time Little Dorrit is 13 she is housekeeper and 'mother' to her brothers and sisters for 'she knew well - no one better - that a man so broken as to be their father of the Marshalsea, could be no father to his own children', and so 'she took the place of eldest of the three in all things but precedence; was the head of the fallen family; and bore in her own heart, its anxieties and shames' (ibid, 1857: 111 & 112).

In Hardy's *Tess of the D'Urbervilles* (1891), the heroine Tess also takes on the role of 'supplementing mother' as her father dies whilst she is in her teens and her mother struggles to rear seven children. Although in this example, Tess is not a primary carer, she is certainly undertaking major familial responsibilities. This raises an important distinction which we wish to emphasise from the outset. Whilst we are principally concerned with the experience of young carers with *prime* responsibility for the caring task, it is important to recognise that, historically and in contemporary society, many children *share* the tasks of caring with adults - often with similar effects on childhood development as experienced by primary young carers.

One must be cautious though of presuming that what is true in fiction is true of society, as Spearman (1966:6) suggests 'the relation between literature and society is not the simple one implied in words like 'product' and 'reflection' so often used to describe it.'

In her work on children in history, McLaughlin suggests that searching for evidence on the true nature of children's lives is problematic considering 'the still unbroken silence that conceals the fortunes of the vast majority of children and parents' (McLaughlin, 1974:139). However, she reports that as far back as the beginning of the 11th Century, there is evidence that due to the early death of one or both parents, young children were turned into the care of older brothers or sisters. Progressing to the 13th Century, McLaughlin notes that life expectancy was around 30 years of age and that those children who survived infancy 'were more likely than not to be orphaned or semi-orphaned at an early age' hence partaking in the care of the family, helping the 'despairing or overburdened mother' (ibid, 1974:101-81).

McLaughlin also points out that those children who were orphaned or found themselves in institutions were often apprenticed or hired out as servants at eight or ten years of age, and even in the 15th and 16th Centuries apprenticeship was common at the standard age of seven. Certainly present day perceptions of the childhood experience are very different from what can be deduced from archival insight, for example children were often sold by their parents because of the severity of their own deprivation and in the 11th and 12th centuries Canon Law suggested the minimum ages for marriage were 12 for girls and 14 for boys.

McLaughlin recounts the example of St Hugh of Lincoln, which provides us with a stark example of the caring process and early father-son relationship. Hugh's mother died early and at the age of eight he joined a community of canons regular with his father. 'As he himself later reported, in "talking confidentially" with his companions "Truly I never tasted the joys of this world. I never knew or learnt how to play...." He often used to relate with great pleasure how for the rest of his father's life, he used to lead him and carry him about, dress and undress him, wash him, dry him and make his bed, and, when he grew feebler and weaker, prepare his food and even feed him' (ibid, 1974:128).

Continuing into the 1800s, the author of *Practical Education*, Maria Edgeworth, was herself a young carer as along with her father Richard Lovell Edgeworth she 'brought up her 16 younger brothers and sisters' (Robertson, 1974: 421).

Recent Studies

The early studies on young carers in the 1980s undoubtedly set the foundations for future research, but gravitated towards quantitative rather than qualitative methods of data collection. This early research also tended to be descriptive rather than analytical in nature. The Sandwell study (Page, 1988) is one such example, the approach as well as the findings reflecting the uncharted nature of this research topic. The Sandwell researchers did not engage in any discussion with the young carers directly, hence we have a somewhat small scale statistical picture, rather than a quality of life ethnographic study based on what young carers themselves are saying about their lives and needs.

The aim of the Sandwell research was to ascertain the extent to which school children were involved in an informal caring role and the impact this had on their lives. However, such effects are difficult to quantify if young carers themselves are not directly involved in the research process through interview or informal discussion. School pastoral staff were asked what they thought the effects of caring would be on a school child. Clearly such an establishment bias inevitably restricts the research to a considerable degree and negates the plausibility of producing a quality of life impression of young caring. However, the Sandwell research was a useful exercise in awareness raising and in providing a provincial summary of the numbers involved.

A further piece of research on young carers is the Tameside study (O'Neill, 1988) but again it adopts a descriptive rather than an interpretative approach. More significantly, it was not designed to focus exclusively on young carers. Indeed young carers comprised only a sub sample of the main carers sample frame, the initial or main study being the Carers Survey for Tameside Social Services Committee. The young carers research was only undertaken following a request by the Association of Carers for some indication of the numbers of young carers, so they could assess and provide for their needs (although it is now clear that assessment and

provision must be informed by more than simple figures). The Tameside researchers recognised that they were only able to provide 'ball park figures' which made it impossible to extrapolate qualitative data on the lives of young carers, and furthermore only provided crude estimates of numbers.

The most recent study specifically focusing on young carers, which adopts a more qualitative approach is the Sefton study (Bilsborrow, 1992). This, more than any previous research provides us with a picture of the experiences and needs of young carers, and indeed for the first time gives young carers a voice. However, if anything this picture is not sufficiently interpretative in that it lacks any real analytical depth. For example, the research adopts Twigg's models of carers (Twigg, 1989) which, although undoubtedly of use when considering the roles of informal carers, are less useful when examining the lives of *children* who care. Their very status as *child* carers sets them apart from the generic 'carer' label. As we have said before and indeed as Twigg and colleagues have suggested (Twigg, Atkin, Perring 1990), it is important to perceive carers *not* as a homogeneous group, but to respect particular distinctions. Thus young carers deserve attention informed by their status as non adult carers - as children. It is clear that there are fundamental differences in the conditions and effects of young caring, which suggest the need to establish and apply new and more appropriate models of caring, relating specifically to age distinctions.

It is important to signal here the work of the Carers National Association Young Carers Project (CNAYCP) funded by the Department of Health, as it has been a cornerstone in awareness raising and enabling and empowering young carers in the community. The Young Carers Project (see Meredith, 1990, 1991a, 1991b, 1991c, 1992) endorses a child-centred view and examines the social impact of caring in terms of the quality of life of young carers. Throughout the CNAYCP literature there is an emphasis on the need to undertake quality of life or investigative study and to avoid further repetition of statistically based research. Such a proposal is based on the view that these young people are 'hidden' carers because of a complex range of factors, including fear and their inability or reluctance to see themselves as 'carers'.

Meredith promotes advocacy and befriending and places a high priority on supporting local development work as a way to address the complex issues surrounding welfare provision for young carers. Meredith has also been instrumental in highlighting the opportunity presented by the Children Act and the Community Care Act as propitious vehicles for putting young caring on the agenda and hence to facilitate service provision. He has also exposed the inappropriate treatment of young carers by the media, who portray them as 'little angels' and the young caring role as a 'triumph over tragedy', whilst ignoring the social and political context that allows young caring to continue, and the costs that are borne by young carers themselves.

The Young Carers Project makes an invaluable contribution to the continuing recognition of young carers as a distinct group of carers. Initially it drew on the Sandwell and Tameside findings to make national estimates of the extent of young caring. Its work has since extended to coordinating research development and offering membership and a contact point for children and young people. Their work also includes the provision of policy consultation for local authorities, and support and advice to workers in contact with young carers.

A Medical Literature
There is a body of medical literature relating to specific illnesses and disabilities which adopts the care receiver's perspective, or focuses on the care receiver's disorder, but which incorporates children who care because of the nature of the particular medical condition. Such work is most apposite in addressing the experiences and needs of the child as carer and the child at risk (both from the effects of early caring and the risks of disease).

Because of the severity of certain disorders and their physiological effects on adults, the impact on the family as a unit - and therefore the child/ren - is considerable. For example, where Parkinson's Disease affects a parent in the family environment, it has a subsequent impact on the child/ren (see Grimshaw, 1991). Where Huntington's Chorea is present the consequences in terms of the effects on the child/ren are considerably more complex (see Harper 1986; Tyler,1990). In these cases the nature of the disease enforces action on the part of both medical and welfare professionals. It inevitably imposes a child-centred view, and it seems that the more severe the condition, the more attention is focused on those affected by it.

In the case of Huntington's Chorea -

'perhaps the most serious disorder of adult life that faces the medical geneticist' (Harper, 1986:7) - there is serious concern for the child, not only because of the indirect effects of having to care for a parent with the disease (Huntington's can cause unpredictable behaviour which can lead to neglect even of basic needs, physical, emotional even sexual abuse - Tyler, 1990), but also the direct effects of the hereditary nature of the condition (there is a one in two chance of the child of an affected parent contracting this wasting disease for which there is no known cure). For these many complex and critical reasons, the child's welfare must be considered.

Although it seems that the child, in the case of Huntington's Chorea, becomes part or potential client, there is recognition of the impact of transmission (genetic counselling, the provision of information, when to tell, who to tell etc; see Tyler, 1990) but there is also consideration of the role the child undertakes as carer. Tyler for example highlights the effects of Huntington's and how it can compromise the parental role, resulting in stressful home conditions and an extra burden of responsibility on the child.

Thus, it is important to recognise that the nature and severity of the adult's illness or disability is not only a determining factor in the emotional or physical effects on the child, but also on the level of responsibilities (ie caring) the child must undertake. Tyler stresses the importance of adopting a family viewpoint. She also recognises the stresses involved for children who care and she makes recommendations which address these tensions.

In his examination of the effects on children of parental alcoholism, Stafford (1992) also recognises the incidence of role reversal between parent and child and the burden of undertaking extra caring responsibilities, the effects of which in this case seem somewhat extreme: 'The child may take responsibility for the poor parenting by supporting and supplementing the parents' parenting. Children become mini parents because they feel that it is their fault that things are not better. These situations can lead to incestuous relationships as the role of sub-stitute parent is taken to its logical conclusion' (ibid, 1992:54). This extreme view was not supported by any evidence in our findings.

Grimshaw (1991) focuses specifically on the child's perspective where Parkinson's Disease afflicts a parent. He too acknow-ledges the role reversal of parent/child relationships and gains considerable insight into the lives and experiences of these young people as carers. In adopting a human rights approach he is sensitive to their many needs: to be treated with respect, to be included in discussions with professionals and service providers and to have access to adequate support and information networks.

In terms of the provision of information Honigsbaum's (1991) work on HIV, AIDS and children is particularly relevant. The focus of this research is the child as client (ie, the child with HIV/AIDS) and not the child as carer. However, the examination of the child's needs - in terms of being heard, inclusion in discussions and the provision of information - is directly relevant to children who are also involved in the caring process.

It is clear that such medical literature is most appropriate in terms of the needs of young carers generally. However, one criticism which could be levelled at such research would be that it tends to talk abstractly about issues rather than directly *with* young people about their experiences.

A Literature of Omission

There is a considerable body of literature which examines carers *per se* and which covers a wide range of topics and perspectives. Variables such as gender, kinship, and race have been examined, but so far age as a factor has been largely neglected. Fallon (1990) notices: 'In the...literature on informal carers, there are few references to children in the caring role.' This is what we have termed a 'literature of omission'.

Certain texts have examined specific *features* of caring, for example daughters who care (Lewis and Meredith, 1988); women (Finch and Groves, 1983); ethnicity (Shah, 1992; Williams, 1990). There is also a wide range of literature concerning *services* for carers (Brimblecombe and Russell, 1988; Twigg, 1990) as well as on the *costs* of caring (Glendinning, 1990 and 1992 ; White 1989). The introduction of new legislation, in particular the NHS and Community Care Act has also brought with it an abundance of research, information and misinformation (Audit Commission, 1992; Beardshaw and Towell, 1990) and yet the issues and voices of young carers remains silent in the flow of discourse. The House of Commons Social Services Committee report on Carers (1990) also fails to refer to young carers despite the many references to the Carers National Association in the report.

Twigg *et al* (1990) have also noted the exclusion of young carers in the current literature. Furthermore they have recognised common factors in the literature on informal carers, that is that carers are perceived as either features of themselves, features of their dependants or features of relationships. The authors suggest that in future research, distinctions need to be respected and examined as specific features in their own right, for example male, elderly or child carers, 'Carers should no longer be treated as quite so homogeneous a group as has been the practice so far' (ibid, 1990:8).

As we have already noted, precious little work focuses specifically on the needs of young carers. Furthermore, considering the lack of awareness of the issue at a local level (see chapter 7) as well as nationally (neither service provision or current legislation includes reference to or discussion of young carers) it is imperative that we first fully understand the experiences and needs of children who care if we are then to adequately provide for their needs.

Conclusion

It is clear that the literature focusing specifically on young carers is extremely limited. Research so far has generally been descriptive in content, focusing on statistical data collection. The qualitative work which has been undertaken either lacks any real analytical depth or employs a single 'snapshot' perspective.

Until now, there has been little attempt to develop any specific analytical models to assist understanding of the young carer's role and needs. There has been no development of a coherent policy agenda for young carers.

Introduction

In the following chapters we will be looking at the lifestyles and experiences of 15 children who care in Nottingham. First, we present the **profiles** of the young carers; introduce each child individually in order to provide an overview of their lives and circumstances. These profiles include a brief summary of the young carers circumstances and a brief comment on the interview process - how the young carer reacted to being interviewed in depth. Our study aims to give young carers a voice. Their individual accounts and the use of their own words are prominent throughout the report.

In chapter three we examine the particular **caring tasks** undertaken by all the young carers: personal, domestic, health and social care. We also look in some detail at their intimate caring responsibilities and the potential effects that such personal task performance may have on their lives and the lives of their loved ones.

Chapter four focuses on the **provision and availability of 'informal' and 'formal' support**. Informal (unpaid) support includes immediate family members, and the network of relatives, friends and neighbours. Formal (paid) support includes professionals from health, education, social services and voluntary agencies. We then examine young carers' attitudes towards these various forms of support.

In chapter five we examine the **effects of caring** in terms of the young carers' home life, social life, and the physical and emotional effects of caring - for example we look at crises, grief and aspirations for the future. We also discuss the effects of caring on the caring

relationship: between the care 'providers' and care 'receivers'.

Chapter six focuses on the **expressed needs of young carers**, both practical and emotional. Having examined in depth the lives and experiences of young carers, we turn our attention in chapter seven to the **attitudes of paid professionals** towards young caring.

In chapter eight we present some **conclusions and principles, guidelines and approaches for action** on the basis of the findings, suggesting proposals for the future care and support of young carers in the community.

Children Who Care - Profiles

In this section we refer briefly to the profiles of the young carers (see Tables 2.1 and 2.2); we then focus on the young carer's individual circumstances. This is followed by a discussion of the contributory factors involved in 'informal' young caring as well as the issues surrounding notions of choice and socialisation (see Box 1).

As Tables 2.1 and 2.2 illustrate, the young carer profiles are divided between young carers whose ages range between three and 18 (Table 2.1), and those adult carers who have cared since childhood, whose ages range between 22 and 35 (Table 2.2).

It was considered important to examine the lives and experiences of the adult carers who had cared since childhood, as they served as a useful comparison with the children currently caring, and lent perspective to the young caring experience. Talking to adult carers also served to highlight the long-term outcomes of young caring.

Table 2.1 Profile of Young Carers and their Families

Carer Details

	Alison	Zia	Mansour	Manoj	Claire	Jas	Debra	Sarah	Diane	Caroline	Jimmy
Age	18	14	12	15	16	15	16	15	17	3yrs	16
Country of Birth	England	England	England	England	Scotland	England	England	England	England	England	England
Ethnicity	White European	Asian	Asian	Asian	White European	Asian	White European	White European	White European	White European	White European
Care for	Mother	Mother & Father	Mother & Father	Mother & Father	Mother	Mother & Father	Mother	Mother	Mother	Grandmother	Mother & Father*
How long providing care	9 yrs	"since able to"	"since able to"	5 yrs	3 yrs	"ages"	3 yrs	3 yrs manifold care	9 yrs	As long as able	Mother 1 yr Father 2 yrs
Age started caring	9	"since able to"	"since able to"	10	12	Since can remember	12	"since a child" 3 yrs manifold care	8	Imprecise	14
Current education	FE College	Secondary school	Secondary school	Secondary school	Awaiting college place	Secondary school**	N/A	Not attending	FE College	N/A	N/A
Current work	P/time Co-op cashier	N/A	N/A	N/A	N/A	N/A	Looking	N/A	N/A	N/A	Trainee chef

Person Cared For

	Alison	Zia	Mansour	Manoj	Claire	Jas	Debra	Sarah	Diane	Caroline	Jimmy
Relationship to carer	Mother	Mother & Father	Mother & Father	Mother & Father	Mother	Mother & Father	Mother	Mother	Mother	Grandmother	Mother Father*
Illness/ disability	Multiple Sclerosis	Osteoporosis arthritis	Osteoporosis arthritis	Arthritis kidney transplant	No diagnosis but immobile	Many heart disease	Huntingtons Chorea	Multiple Sclerosis	Multiple Sclerosis	Rheumatoid & osteo arthritis, hiatus hernia	Mother Stroke + heart attack Father brain tumour*
Current work	p/time day centre	None	None	None	None	None	None	None	None	None	None
Housing	Own bungalow	Own house	Own house	?	Council House	Own house	Grandmother's council house	Council house	Own house	Council bungalow	Council bungalow

Family Members

	Alison	Zia	Mansour	Manoj	Claire	Jas	Debra	Sarah	Diane	Caroline	Jimmy
Brother	None	One, younger 12	One, older 14	One	One, younger 4	Three, younger 14, older 17 & 21	Stepbrother younger 4	Two, twin 15, (older 23~)	None	Mother pregnant	Two, (older 22 & 24~)
Sister	None	None	None	One	One, younger 13	Three, younger 11, older 19 & 20	None	One older 21	None	None	One, younger 11
Parents	Mother	Mother & Father	Mother & Father	Mother & Father	Mother	Mother & Father	None at home	Mother & Father	Mother	Mother & Father	Mother
Grandparents	None at home	None at home	None at home	None at home	None at home	None at home	Grandmother	None at home	None at home	Grandmother	None at Home

* Now Deceased   **Expelled   ~ Not living in the family home

Table 2.2	Profile of Young Carers (Now Adults) and their Families			
Carer Details				
	Linda	**Gary**	**Miriam**	**Sally**
Age	22	22	29	35
Country of birth	England	England	England	England
Ethnicity	White European	White European	White European	White European
Current work	Secretary	Volunteer	Carer	Carer
Housing	Rented Trust	Parents own	Parent's Council	Council
Care for	Mother*	Brother (age 17)	Mother	Mother
How long providing care	5-6 months full time	17 years	14 years	23 years
Age started caring	18	5	15	12
Person cared For				
Relationship to carer	Mother	Brother	Mother	Mother
Illness/disability	Breast cancer	Brain damage at birth	Multiple Sclerosis	Rheumatoid arthritis
Work	N/A	None	None	None
Family Members Living at Home				
Spouse	Single	Single	Single	Husband
Son	None	None	None	None
Daughter	None	None	None	One, 2 years
Parents	None at home	Mother & Father	Mother & Father	Mother
Siblings	None at home	Brother	None at Home	None at Home

* Now Deceased

Tables 2.1 and 2.2 provide a comprehensive overview of the circumstances and conditions of the young and adult carers and their families. Interestingly, nine out of the 15 young carers were female (reinforcing Braithwaite's (1992) assertion that care givers are usually women, and Bilsborrow's (1992) findings), and only one out of the 15 was solely responsible for a male care receiver. Notably, the majority of male young carers were from minority ethnic communities. As there has been very little work carried out on young carers from these communities it is not possible from these findings to assert that in Asian families, for example, caring responsibilities are *usually* undertaken by male children. McCalman (1990:37) suggests, however, that the Asian community often expects family members to care for relatives without external support and intervention.

The median age of the young carers was 15, and the average starting age for care (excluding three year old Caroline) was between eight and nine for the young carers and 12 for those young carers who are now adult carers. However, these figures are somewhat imprecise because many of the young carers could not be categorical about their age when caring responsibilities began.

The nature and extent of the care receiver's illness or disability was a determining factor on the level of caring responsibilities undertaken by the young carers. These illnesses were all long-term, disabling conditions, many of which became severe over time, and all of which would have profound impacts on the lives of children who care.

Individual Case Studies

All names used are pseudonyms.

Alison is 18 and an only child. She lives in a village outside Nottingham where she cares for her mother who has multiple sclerosis. Alison's father died suddenly when she was nine. She is studying hairdressing at a local college and has a Saturday job in a local supermarket. Alison and her mother live together in a small bungalow where Alison does all the housework, prepares meals and works in the garden which is her 'pride and joy'. Her mother works part time as a clerk at a local day centre. Although Alison has cared for her mother for some considerable time, her mother's disability is increasing and Alison is responsible for showering her mother as well as various other personal tasks. Alison clearly suffered a great deal when her father died and her mother became ill. She experienced a long period of rebellion.

During interviews: Alison was initially very shy, but she gradually became more willing to talk. However, she was always conscious that she could not express herself very well and worried that she was not being very helpful. At the end of the first interview she said she wanted to help others in her situation and would be willing to help further in the research.

Zia and Mansour are brothers aged 14 and 12 respectively. They live four miles north of Nottingham with their parents. They care for their parents who have a range of illnesses (both have disabling conditions). Their parents originate from Pakistan and both boys - who attend a local comprehensive school - have been subject to considerable racial abuse in the past (especially at their previous school). Their caring tasks vary and sometimes include the preparation and cooking of meals and domestic duties such as cleaning, dusting, making beds etc. As their parents' conditions progress their caring tasks have increased and have recently included lifting duties for their father who has just been made redundant from work due to his increasing disability.

During interviews: the boys' father was present throughout and both the boys appeared very shy and sometimes restricted by his presence. However, they both seemed mature for their ages and had clear ambitions for the future, which included the continuing care of both parents. Both were aware of the lack of formal support available for the family and were keen to take on major household tasks as they got older.

Manoj is 15 and lives in Nottingham with his parents. He has brothers and sisters but they have left the family home. Manoj cares for his mother and father who have a range of illnesses. He undertakes most of the housework and family shopping and takes his father to and from hospital. He also translates for both parents. Manoj attends a local comprehensive school.

During interviews : Manoj was extremely shy and uncomfortable throughout the first interview and for this reason it was curtailed. His reluctance to talk could have been affected by the presence of his father, and later his sister-in-law. He did not appear to want to talk about his caring responsibilities and responded throughout the interviews in monosyllables.

Claire is 15 and lives in Nottingham in a council owned terraced house with her mother and younger sister and brother. Claire undertakes the primary care of her mother who is disabled with an undiagnosed condition (she is immobile). Claire has been caring since she was 13 and undertakes domestic tasks as well as carrying her mother up and down stairs, washing and dressing her. Claire has left school and is awaiting a place at a local college to study nursing. There is little money coming into the house which has been seriously neglected.

During Interviews: Claire appeared to be staunchly independent and did not want any outside 'interference'. She became very aggressive when discussing professionals or 'authority figures', but she openly talked about her caring experiences. However, she would not talk about her financial situation, or how the family manages with so little money coming in.

Jas is 15 and lives in a terraced house in Nottingham with his parents, one older brother and a younger brother and sister. Jas undertakes the majority of caring tasks for both parents, but mainly for his father who is confined to bed with a range of illnesses. Jas's caring responsibilities include dressing his father, administering medicines, taking him to hospital and carrying out domestic tasks. He also translates for both parents. Jas was attending a local comprehensive school, but has been expelled.

During interviews: Jas was initially very shy (indeed he ran out of the room at the start of the interview, but was persuaded to come back), but he soon talked openly about his caring experiences, despite the presence of his sick father and his mother and sister. Jas said he didn't particularly enjoy his caring role and had run away from home on several occasions, but he always came back it seems because of a sense of duty to his family.

Debra is 17 and lives on a council estate three miles west of the city centre. She lives with her maternal grandmother. Until recently Debra was caring for her mother who has Huntington's Chorea. Her mother has since been institutionalised as her condition deteriorated and she was becoming violent towards Debra. Debra cared for her mother since the age of nine during which time her father left home. For a brief time Debra lived with her mother and step father but he became violent and eventually he also left. Debra has had a very disruptive and often violent life with her mother and was relieved when they were eventually separated. Debra used to undertake all the domestic tasks in the house as well as personal hygiene tasks for her mother. Debra has left school and is trying to find a job in hairdressing. She understands that she has a one in two chance of contracting Huntingtons Chorea, but does not want to find out for sure through genetic testing. The relationship with her grandmother is very strained as Debra likes to go out and her grandmother tries to stop her. Her grandmother also has a heart condition.

During interviews: Initially Debra was upset because she had just received a job rejection. She found it difficult to recall her past at times because she seemed confused about the caring sequence. However, she talked openly about her caring experiences in general and often elicited anger that she had been left alone to cope with her mother for such a long time. She seemed to resent her mother's illness and her inability to look after Debra properly. She no longer visited her mother in the home.

Sarah is 15 and lives in a council house four miles west of the city. She lives with her parents, twin brother and older sister but she undertakes the main caring responsibilities (although her father cooks all the meals). Sarah's mother has multiple sclerosis. Sarah showers, toilets and dresses her mother and carries out some domestic tasks. Sarah has not attended school for two years due to a row between her father and the school authorities. She cannot read or write. She also suffered some emotional problems after being attacked by several boys outside her previous school.

During interviews: Sarah was very willing to talk about her caring experiences and seemed to want someone to talk to about her problems. She seemed to be very close to her mother and remained in the house with her most of the time, going out rarely. She said she wanted to nurse the elderly as a career but realised she must learn to read and write and pass exams before she could do so.

Diane is 17 and lives in a terraced house two miles south of the city with her mother who has multiple sclerosis. Diane is an only child and has cared for her mother since she was eight when her father left home. Diane undertakes all of the domestic tasks and some personal caring responsibilities for her mother. Diane attends a local college where she is studying for her A levels. She is uncertain about her career ambitions, but she does not intend to leave her mother.

During interviews: Diane was more than willing to talk about her experiences and seemed to cope well with her caring responsibilities. She seemed to be very close to her mother, although she said they sometimes argue because they are together most of the time. Diane has access to quite a wide support network of friends and neighbours.

Caroline is three years old and lives in a council bungalow three miles west of the city. She lives with her parents and grandmother who is disabled. It was very difficult to communicate with Caroline and the details about her caring responsibilities were obtained from her mother and grandmother. Caroline assists in feeding her grandmother and generally 'fetches and carries' for her. As her mother intends to have another child, the family believe that Caroline's duties will increase.

Jimmy is 17 and lives with his mother and younger sister in a council bungalow three miles west of the city. He is currently on work experience as a trainee chef at a local restaurant. Jimmy's mother has a heart condition and has suffered several strokes, but Jimmy does not undertake primary caring responsibilities for her as he does not get along with the family. He was placed with his mother (reluctantly) following his father's recent death from a brain tumour. Jimmy nursed his dying father on his own for two years, as his mother had left home taking his

sister with her. Caring for his father was a very traumatic experience for Jimmy as he was very close to him and was devastated when he died. Jimmy refused to attend school while he was caring for his father. They had very little money, were prosecuted for trying to defraud the DSS and taken to court for non school attendance (his father was fined, Jimmy was put on probation). Jimmy had to beg for food parcels and was having to undertake domestic and personal tasks for his father. He also had to take him to hospital and cope with his fits which were a consequence of the brain tumour. Throughout the caring period, no one offered any constructive support either to Jimmy or his father, and Jimmy was afraid he would be separated from him. When his father died, Jimmy was offered the choice of going to live with his mother or being put into care.

During interviews: Jimmy was initially very shy and embarrassed, but eventually he began to talk openly about his experiences in some considerable detail. This was the first time he had ever spoken about his past, his caring role and his father and by the end of the interview he was visibly distressed. He clearly misses his father a great deal and is very unhappy in his present circumstances. He is still angry that he was left to cope alone with his father and that no one talked to him about his caring role or how to cope.

Linda is 22 and lives with her older brother in a rented bungalow four miles north of the city. Linda works as a secretary at a local university. Until recently she cared for her mother who had breast cancer (but who has since died). Linda's father left home when she was 13, and shortly afterwards her mother's condition was diagnosed. She began caring for her when she was nearly 18 and the level of care increased as her mother's condition deteriorated. For the last five or six months of her mother's life she was caring for her full time including domestic and personal tasks. Her brother helped with caring tasks when he could, but the main responsibility fell on Linda's shoulders.

During interviews: Linda was very willing to talk about her caring responsibilities and about her mother, although she clearly still misses her a great deal. Linda was very willing to take on her caring role, but it was clearly very distressing for her.

Gary is 23 and lives with his parents and younger brother in a village south of Nottingham. Gary cares for his younger brother who was brain damaged at birth and is both physically and mentally disabled. Gary has cared for him for 17 years (since his brother was born) because of 'a special bond' between them. Gary is currently looking for paid work although he works as a volunteer at a local centre for the 'physically and mentally handicapped'. Although Gary's parents are willing and able to care, Gary undertakes many of the caring responsibilities including toileting, dressing and entertaining his brother.

During interviews: Gary was initially shy, but soon talked openly about his caring experiences. He clearly loves his brother very much and enjoys caring for him. However, caring became difficult when his mother went into hospital for six months and his father spent most of his time visiting her, leaving Gary to care for his brother alone. Gary has also suffered from Myalgic Encephalomyelitis (ME) which meant he often felt too tired to care for his brother. However, Gary has willingly committed himself to a 'lifetime' of caring for his brother.

Miriam is 29 and lives with her parents in a rented bungalow in Nottingham. Miriam left school at 16 to take up the full time care of her mother (she receives Invalid Care Allowance) who has multiple sclerosis. Miriam's father works and does not undertake any of the caring responsibilities. Consequently Miriam carries out all the domestic and personal tasks for her mother, which she started when she was still at school. Miriam has brothers and sisters who have left home and who give Miriam very little support. She has very few friends and rarely socialises. Her life is centred on the family home and the care of her mother.

During interviews: Miriam was very willing to talk about her caring experiences. Her relationship with her mother is volatile and she does not get on with her father. If anything, Miriam seemed somewhat resentful of her caring role, especially as she received little appreciation for her work from the rest of the family. Miriam was looking ahead to a time when she no longer had to care for her mother (ie when her mother dies or is hospitalised).

Sally is 35 and lives with her husband, mother and two year old daughter in a rented bungalow three miles west of the city. She cares for her mother who is disabled with rheumatoid arthritis. She has cared for her mother for 23 years, and when she was a child managed her caring responsibilities on her own. Sally currently receives outside nursing support for her mother, but she still has to feed and dress her as well as wash her and prepare her meals.

During interviews: Sally was happy to talk about her caring responsibilities which have become less of a burden with age. She seemed to be quite close to her mother, but her mother was present throughout the interview which could have prevented Sally from talking more openly about the relationship.

Box One

Choice and Socialisation

It is important to outline some of the factors that help determine the nature and extent of young caring. So far we have presented the profiles and conditions of the young carers involved in the research, but it is essential to indicate a factor which can exacerbate the stress of caring (and indeed influence the level of care provided) and which in turn affects the young carers' access to choice. This factor is money, which more than any other external dynamic affects the reality of young caring.

The majority of the young carers interviewed experienced economic privations. Their families were either living off one wage, or social security benefits, and as the children could not contribute to the family income, then neither could they refuse to undertake a role which lack of money had forced on them. We found no evidence of young carers who had *chosen* to undertake the caring role or who were given any effective alternatives. Furthermore, none of the young carers demonstrated any understanding of the concept of choice in relation to their caring roles.

It was clear from the findings that neither personal feelings or caring options were involved in the young carers' decision to undertake the caring role. Many of these young carers had been coerced - whether emotionally or practically - into caring, and had been caring for as long as they could remember. We can say that they have been 'socialised' into their caring roles.

Lewis and Meredith (1988) identified certain vocabulary and 'triggers' in their research on adult carers - that people took a 'conscious decision' to care or became 'reluctantly involved'. The triggers for the young carers were entirely enforced by economic deprivation and specific circumstances, such as the separation of parents and/or the onset of illness/disability, coupled with the lack of outside support and their convenient availability as child helpers in the house. This is not meant to imply that care receivers are exploiting child labour: they too have little choice in appropriating their children for caring duties.

Evidence of socialisation into care can be found in many of the young carers' experience of the inception of care. For some of the children the rigours of caring were not dissimilar from the stresses and strains already present in their home lives. For example Debra said:

No I didn't have any choice, but it was like I was used to it. Like my life had been rough anyway, so it was no change.

Young carers demonstrated resignation and acceptance of their caring roles, due to their early socialisation. For example, Debra commented:

I didn't feel as if I had any choice, but it didn't bother me - I'd been used to it since I was so young. Sometimes it gets to you - not very often cos I'm used to it.

Socio-economic deprivation influenced the young carers' acquiescence, and the lack of formal or voluntary support meant the burden of emotional and practical responsibility fell entirely on their shoulders. As no caring alternatives were offered, they were forced into emotional reconciliations between love and a sense of duty - and neglect would be the outcome of their refusal to care. For example: 'He's my dad isn't he - you can't just leave him' (Jas). This theme recurred constantly.

Another influencing factor in relation to choice, or the power to choose, is the young carers' status as children. Two issues are involved here: maturity and evaluation. A child is judged a child in all aspects of life: educationally, socially, medically and in law they are managed as children with few powers and no access to choice - 'children are the least powerful social group' (Alderson 1992:163). In the home as young carers, however, their 'adult' responsibilities are conferred on them. Thus their power to choose in terms of caring is undermined even further. Even as young carers in the home, power is denied them, their role conferred on them - and yet it is precisely in the home where they are in effect the adults of the house in terms of the nature of their duties and responsibilities.

Evaluation is a significant factor which because young carers have often adapted to their role over time (have been socialised into it), they have no tools available with which to evaluate their lives and reconstruct or reject their caring roles, or accept any notion of choice. They often have no other life pattern with which to compare their own, unlike adult carers who can evaluate their caring options through the channels of the past.

Conclusion

Young carers are effectively denied the prospect of choice and often circumstances (usually socio economic) prevail in the home to prevent the activation of caring alternatives. However, these issues combined do not seem to affect the young carers' feelings towards their parent/s or their commitment to continue in the caring role. Indeed, the level of affection and commitment demonstrated (mostly under very trying and painful circumstances) was particularly striking. What is needed is for this love and affection to be allowed to preside without the added burdens and strains of caring; to allow young carers the freedom of choice; to give them a voice; to provide for them so that they are not forced to be their parents' parents.

3 Caring Tasks and Responsibilities

Introduction

The performance of tasks and caring responsibilities was the most commonly discussed subject among the young and adult carers. The fact that task performance occupied most of their time and attention no doubt accounts for this focus. For most young carers their lives were a constant performance of domestic and personal caring labours.

Most of the young carers started caring at a very young age (see Tables 2.1 and 2.2) their responsibilities increasing as they got older. However, it is important to emphasise that the level and intensity of caring tasks is very much determined by the nature and severity of the care receiver's illness or disability. For example, the level of care involved for Debra (who cared for her mother with Huntington's Chorea) was far more intense than the level of care for Gary (whose parents were both able to supplement the care of his brother) or Alison, whose mother worked part-time and was determined to exert her independence as far as possible. Debra's mother's condition required a great deal of intimate caring as her condition meant she had to be toileted, washed and dressed and eventually she required 24-hour care.

The level of task performance was also determined by the availability of outside help, which we will examine in chapter four. However, all the young carers were undertaking primary caring roles, with the exception of Gary who only provided primary care intermittently.

The Nature and Extent of Caring Tasks

The level of tasks performed by the young carers ranged from basic domestic chores

(washing up, making drinks) to personal intimate tasks including washing, toileting and dressing the care receiver. Other less common tasks were also evident. These often caused considerable distress for the young carers. For example Jimmy had cared for his father for some years, managing the effects of his brain tumour (which included fits) as well as performing a wide range of intimate tasks for him. Finally, when his father died Jimmy also had to arrange his funeral, without any outside support or comfort.

Jimmy and the other children who were caring for a parent with a chronic condition, provided the most intense levels of care. To an 'outsider' these tasks might seem at least very distressing and at worst quite repugnant. It was perhaps Zia and Mansour who performed the most basic level of care (although this would undoubtedly increase as they got older and their parents' disability increased) but they were able to enjoy the support of their parents: their parents tried as far as possible to limit the burden of their responsibilities.

What was perhaps striking was the young carers' fortitude and acceptance of their caring roles. As the following examples illustrate, the young carers - socialised from an early age into their caring roles - acknowledged and defined their various duties (many of them of an intimate nature) as everyday routines. As they listed their caring responsibilities they did so without any sign of complaint or distress:

> *Well, she's got a catheter in so I just have to empty the bag.*
> (Miriam)

*Well I'm sort of lazy really I've got to say
it, I help her to the toilet, shower her,
stuff like that.*

(Sarah)

*To help my dad out I dress him, take him
to the toilet, keep him warm, listen for
him in the night, give him medicines,
watch him because when he smokes he
drops his fags on the floor, he might set
light to himself.*

(Jas)

*I would get up, get a wash, put the kettle
on, get a bowl of water, sponge, soap, give
my mum a wash, get her dressed, go and
get something from the shop for her,
brush her hair and teeth.*

(Debra).

In order to better understand the range of
tasks the young carers were undertaking, we
used a verbal questionnaire which had been
adapted from the National Association of
Health Authorities and Trusts (NAHAT)
categories of health and social care. Caring
tasks are divided into health care, social care
and those that fall into both categories. We
adapted these categories in order to define
and classify the responsibilities involved in
young caring.

Young carers were heavily involved in
both domestic and personal task performance
(see Tables 3.1 and 3.2) and mostly in the
social care category, although there was some
crossover. It was also evident that the adult
carers who had cared since childhood
performed more domestic tasks (see Tables
3.3 and 3.4) and perhaps more so than the

young carers, although the figures are very
small. (It is important to remember that the
level of task performance referred to caring at
the time of interview). It must also be stressed
that because a young carer responded
negatively to a particular question did not
necessarily imply that someone else
performed that specific task, it was more
likely that the task wasn't carried out at all.

Furthermore, the questions adapted from
the NAHAT questionnaire do in themselves
impose a standard of 'normal' practice which
might not necessarily apply to young carers.
For example, one young carer when asked
about washing floors responded: 'I don't
believe in it'. A further example was when
Jimmy said he did not pay bills in person, not
because someone else paid them, but because
they had no money to pay them at all.

In terms of gardening, ironing, and
cleaning windows, the general response was
that these were superfluous and unnecessary
tasks.

Tables 3.1 to 3.4 provide a general
categorisation of the level and nature of tasks
performed by the young carers. What the
tables *don't* reveal is probably just as
significant as what they do reveal.

Jimmy's case is significant here in that
domestic duties such as cleaning became
redundant exercises when compared to the
degree of attention his father required.
Certain domestic tasks became irrelevant as
Jimmy struggled to provide intimate care for
his father. The amount of domestic duties
required in addition to his personal care was
too much for him:

In the end the house got such a tip

Table 3.1	Commonality of Domestic Tasks Performed by the Young Carers				
Domestic task Social care:	No. of young carers	Domestic task Health care:	No. of young carers	Domestic task Health/Social care:	No. of young carers
Light cleaning	9	Collect prescription	8	Empty/clean commode	2
Making drinks	9				
Make/change beds	8				
Washing up	8				
Heavy cleaning	8				
Washing clothes	7				
Prepare meals	7				
Cook meals	7				
Shopping/ shopping assistance	6				
Organising heating	5				
Gardening	5				
Washing floors	4				
Ironing	4				
Pay bills in person	4				
Bank transactions	3				
Clean windows inside	2				

Note: The number of young carers was 11

Table 3.2 Commonality of Personal Tasks Performed by the Young Carers

Personal Task Social Care:	No. of young carers	Personal Task Health Care:	No. of young carers	Personal Task/ Health care:	No. of young carers
Sit listen/personal interest	9	Lift sitting position in bed	4	Dressing/ Undressing assistance	5
Assisting mobility indoors	7	Lift upstairs	3	Assisting to shower	5
Assisting mobility outdoors	5	Feeding assistance	3	Assisting to bath	4
Hair care	4	Lift onto toilet	2	Washing face/hands	4
Manicure	4	Reinforce rehabilitation exercises	2	Assisting to toilet	4
Pedicure	4			Administer tablets	4
Lift in/out bath	3			Rising/tucking in assistance	3
				Clean after continence/ evacuation	3
				Encourage social skills	2
				Applying inco pads	1
				Bagging inco pads	1

Note: The number of young carers was 11

Table 3.3	Commonality of Domestic Tasks Performed by the Four Young Carers (Now Adults)					
Domestic Task Social Care:	No. of Carers	Domestic Task Health Care	No. of Carers	Domestic task Social/Health Care	No. of Carers
Make/change bed	4	Collect Prescription	4	Empty/clean commode	2
Clean windows inside	4				
Washing up	4				
Washing clothes	4				
Shopping/ Shopping assistance	4				
Pay Bills in person	4				
Bank transactions	4				
Prepare meals	4				
Cook meals	4				
Make drinks	4				
Light cleaning	4				
Heavy cleaning	4				
Washing floors	4				
Organising heating	3				
Ironing	3				

Note: The maximum number of young carers (now adults) was four

Table 3.4	Commonality of Personal Tasks Performed by the Four Young Carers (Now Adults)					
Personal Task Social Care	No. of Carers	Personal Task Health Care	No. of Carers	Personal Task Health/Social Care	No. of Carers
Hair care	4	Feeding assistance	4	Dressing/ undressing assistance	4
Sit listen/personal interest	4	Reinforce rehabilitation exercises	3	Administer tablets	4
Assisting mobility outdors	4	Lift onto toilet	2	Washing face/hands	4
Manicure	3	Lift sitting position in bed	1	Rising/tucking in assistance	2
Pedicure	3	Lift in/out bath	0	Applying inco pads	2
Assisting mobility indoors	3			Bagging inco pads	2
Lift upstairs	0			Assit to toilet	2
				Assisting to bath	2
				Assisting to shower	2
				Clean after continence/ evacuation	2
				Encourage social skills	0

Note: The maximum number of young carers (now adults) was four

*upstairs that one room was totally closed
off. I thought why not put everything in
the bin? I cleared out the living room,
cleared out the kitchen and that was it - I
could cope with the house then.*
(Jimmy)

As Tables 3.1 and 3.2 indicate, the most
frequently performed duties were light
domestic tasks such as cleaning, making
drinks, washing up etc. Over half the young
carers also carried out meal preparation and
cooking duties. Such tasks may not seem
excessive and indeed children in non-carer
households may also be undertaking such
tasks. However, the frequency and duration
of such tasks, coupled with the potential
dangers (for instance in cooking meals)
suggests that a disproportionate burden is
placed on young carers.

The Tables do not demonstrate
intermittent task performance either. For
example, some of the young carers, although
mostly exempt from regular meal
preparation, had to undertake such duties at
certain times, for example when the care
receiver was particularly ill or had an illness
in addition to their permanent one.

Some of the young carers, such as Debra,
were more heavily involved in domestic
responsibilities:

*From the age of nine I was doing all the
dinners and everything - I shouldn't have
been doing all that.*
(Debra)

Furthermore, Debra's decision to
undertake the cooking was forced on her

because her mother had 'chucked out the
meals on wheels'.

Clearly, tasks such as meal preparation
had considerable impact on the young carers'
lives both socially and educationally. For
example, Alison prepared all the meals in
advance in her spare time and then froze
them. She also came home from school at
lunch times to cook for herself and her
mother. She also prepared the evening meals.
Furthermore, for Alison it was not simply a
matter of preparing, freezing and cooking the
meals later, but also planning in advance
what they were going to eat. It was often the
planning stages which took up much of her
time and thought.

It was more difficult to define caring
responsibilities in terms of health and social
care of a domestic or personal nature when
the care receiver's condition was so severe to
demand 24-hour attention, as was the case for
both Jimmy and Debra. Jimmy clearly found
it difficult (aside from the yes and no
questionnaire responses) to distinguish
between the performance of tasks and his
emotional responses to his father's needs.
Some tasks were simply not quantifiable. For
example, when he tried to instil 'fighting
spirit' into his father:

*I was getting frustrated with him, you
know I couldn't believe that he was going
to die. I was trying to get him to have a
bit of a fight, I couldn't bear to see him, a
manhat size couldn't lift his hands they
were all crumpled.*
(Jimmy)

The situation was considerably less

complex for those young carers whose level of caring was successfully accommodated around school or college, such as Zia, Mansour, Jas and Diane. However, even here there are 'hidden elements of care'. For example, Diane spent some considerable time planning and organising care for her mother in Diane's absence, ensuring her mother was not entirely alone during the hours Diane was at college. Claire also tried to ensure that neighbours and friends would 'keep an eye on' her mother while Claire was at school. Others did not have access to any outside support and were forced to leave their parents unattended throughout the day:

Before she was in a wheelchair, when I was at school, once she came downstairs, she just stayed in the kitchen all day.
(Miriam)

Many of the young carers took time off school to care for their parent/s (see chapter five), not only because there were times when their parent's needed them at home, but also because of the latent anxiety caused by the young carers' knowledge that their parent/s were alone all day, sometimes trapped in one room of the house.

In terms of effects it is clear that at the very least, task performance is time consuming. Such tasks might not specifically prevent young carers for example from doing their homework, but they inevitably restrict the time many non-carers for instance might spend on play, education, sporting or social activities. (In chapter five we examine the effects of caring on such aspects of young carers lives). A hidden element of the young

carers role is the planning of care - meals etc, and the care of their loved ones when the young carer is at school or elsewhere.

Defining physical tasks was a less complex process. Even Caroline who was three years old and could not clearly articulate the nature of her daily tasks, was providing feeding assistance for her grandmother. Caroline's mother said that Caroline would help feed her grandmother on a regular basis and 'wanted to help out, she's always fetching things and carrying things for her as well'.

All the young carers were involved in some physical personal task performance. However, the physical effects of such caring responsibilities caused difficulties, and pain, for the children involved. This was especially true where the young carers were involved in lifting the care receiver. Eight out of the ten young carers (excluding Caroline) had been involved in some form of lifting during the course of care. This fact only emerged through in-depth questioning. For example on face value, Zia performed clearly demarcated domestic tasks. It was only after persistent questioning that it emerged he also had to help his father up from the floor when he was lying down in front of the television because 'he got stuck sometimes'.

This may be an inevitable consequence in a family where severe arthritis is present, but Zia was only 14 (and slightly built) and lifting or supporting people with disabilities is a practice which requires training if injuries are to be avoided. As his father's condition progressed, Zia's lifting responsibilities increased.

Lifting responsibilities were also causing

physical injury or exacerbating existing problems. Among the young carers, lifting tasks ranged from helping a care receiver into the shower, lifting onto the toilet, to physically carrying them up the stairs. For example, Claire carried her disabled mother up two flights of stairs (to the bedroom and to the toilet). She did so by 'giving her a piggy back all the time'. When Claire was not available, her 13 year old sister Susan also gave their mother a 'piggy back'. However, Claire's lifting ability had been seriously affected by a knee injury which she said was not caused by lifting her mother, but which meant further lifting exacerbated the injury causing further damage to her knee, or indeed to her mother:

> I fell with my mum like because I've got a bad knee. I bruised a tendon and had a lot of shit done on my knee and that, so I'm not supposed to carry her, but I still do it.
> (Claire)

Claire had been told by a visiting nurse not to lift her mother, but she had not been offered any alternative nor shown how to lift her properly. Clearly the nurse might have been reluctant to train Claire properly in lifting techniques for fear of condoning such caring duties. However, as we have indicated, Claire was not provided with any suitable alternatives. She had no choice but to continue lifting her mother.

None of the young carers who were involved in lifting had been shown how to do so properly by trained staff. Even when Claire went to the specialist about her knee and she told them she carried her mother up and down stairs 'They just said to me I wasn't doing enough exercise. My own GP said I shouldn't be doing it'.

Claire admitted that her four year old brother also used to help his mother up the stairs:

> When he was about two he used to lift her legs for her to get her up the stairs. Now the little devil he exercisesher legs - even when it's painful, he lifts them and bends them and says 'Mum's got to do her exercises'.

Diane sustained an injury from lifting her mother, which was exacerbated at times of prolonged or frequent lifting ie outside the home environment:

> When she wants to stand up from off the chair or the edge of the bed, then it's a problem because with her only being able to use one arm I'm only able to use one arm because I have trouble with my elbow - it puts strain on it. It starts to ache sometimes when we go on holiday, with it being a strange environment and there's a lot of lifting, lugging mum about, it starts to put strain on me, on my shoulder and elbow.
> (Diane)

Jimmy also encountered severe difficulties lifting his father. Although physically Jimmy was quite strong, his father was 17 stone and Jimmy had to lift him up the stairs to the toilet. Eventually the stair banister broke, which meant Jimmy could no longer support his father up the stairs. Thus his father was confined to the downstairs rooms and because he could not get to the toilet, he often 'messed himself in the chair.'

Personal Intimate Task Performance

The Children Act emphasises the rights of children to be consulted and the need to ascertain their wishes and feelings when making decisions about service provision which affects their lives. Therefore, young carers must have a right to say what they feel about their role as providers of informal personal care, and a right to choose whether they undertake that role.

Few of the young carers interviewed wanted someone to come into their homes and relieve them of their caring duties. Although some of the young carers would have welcomed some form of professional or voluntary support, it would have to be provided or offered sensitively and bearing individual requirements in mind (both the needs of the care receiver and the care provider). It is imperative that young carers are protected from physical harm (for example from lifting) and to ensure the promotion of their civil rights. But first we must seek their views. Understanding their feelings, determining their experiences through direct contact with them will provide 'a way of involving them in deciding the best balance' (see Alderson, 1992:155).

It has been a long-term concern that children should not be exploited as workers and there are laws which specify children should not work past a certain time in the evening. However, if their parent needs toileting or any kind of attention during the night, what alternative do young carers have but to provide that care?

It has also been argued that children need to develop a sense of personal identity and self esteem based on links with family and friends (Alderson 1992:167). To what extent does wiping their parents or toileting them deny young carers' self esteem? What effect do such intimate responsibilities have on their sense of identity? It was clear from the findings that those young carers who had been performing intimate tasks long term, did not elicit high levels of embarrassment in terms of discussing their tasks, but this does not imply that they are comfortable performing such duties.

For the purposes of this research, showering or bathing, toileting, wiping and dressing were identified as the main intimate caring tasks (and potential sources of embarrassment), and which were most likely to undermine the dignity of both care receiver and care provider. These are also responsibilities that non-carer children do not have to perform for their parents (indeed the majority of children would no doubt consider such duties distasteful and distressing).

It is important to determine the nature and extent of young carers' feelings in relation to such intimate responsibilities. For adaptation or socialisation do not necessarily equate with contentment in the intimate caring role. We have to look at levels of embarrassment as well as aspects of human pride and dignity.

These were at the forefront of Miriam's discussion when she related her intimate caring experiences:

I used to hate seeing her naked. I hadn't

seen an older woman like that. I know it's my mother but it's just something you don't do, you don't see your mother naked.

Other tasks which were indirectly intimate in nature, were looked upon with grim resignation and acceptance. For example emptying catheter bags or commodes:

She used to do it into the commode or something and I used to have to empty it and I didn't like that.
(Miriam)

In terms of toileting, it was precisely those young carers who performed such tasks regularly who hated them most. This is perhaps not surprising, for although the young carers had been socialised into their roles from an early age, they had never adapted to wiping their parents after urination or evacuation. Indeed, what was clear was the relentless misery involved for the young carers in performing such tasks. Jimmy is a case in point. He had always admired and respected his father (which was why he chose to stay with him when his parents divorced). To then be forced to witness his father's physical and mental deterioration (due to his brain tumour) was very distressing and painful for him.

His father's loss of control over his bodily functions not only represented the loss of hope for Jimmy (he knew by then his father was seriously ill) but also seemed to epitomise his father's denigration as well as highlight his loss of dignity and pride.

It's horrible having to do that sort of thing for your dad. It's degrading and it was especially degrading for my dad losing control of himself, and then having to be washed and cleaned up by me.

Debra also had to manage her mother's incontinence:

The more the years pile on, the more you have to do because the worse she's getting, like eventually she'd begin to mess herself and stuff like that. I hated that.

Toileting epitomised the most extreme form of intimate caring for the young carers, but other intimate tasks such as showering or dressing assistance were responsibilities for which the young carers demonstrated a remarkable tolerance, so much so that it became as familiar and acceptable as any other task. Both Sarah and Gary had grown accustomed to such roles:

It's something you get used to from a very early age. I had to get used to it, now it doesn't bother me.
(Gary)

Or Sarah:

After a while I just got used to showering my mum. Just one more thing you've got to do. I was embarrassed when she first asked me and for a bit I thought you know Tessa's older [sister] why didn't she ask her, but I just said all right then. You've got to help out.

In terms of the young carers (now adults) it was clear that access to external support, and thus their abilities to choose whether they performed intimate tasks, increased as they progressed from childhood into adulthood. Once they had reached adult 'independence' they were treated more seriously by professionals (see chapter four). Alderson's point is most apposite here: 'Children's autonomy may be denied and their dignity, privacy and any ability to decide their own best interests ignored until they reach adult independence' (Alderson 1992:171).

This was evident from the comparison between adult and young carers. The latter had no choice in performing intimate tasks for their parent/s, the only variable being whether they required that sort of help or not.

The young carers (now adults) had much more access to professional support networks. For example, Linda was able to obtain nursing support for her mother who towards the end of her illness was no longer able to bath herself. As a young carer this task would no doubt have fallen on Linda's shoulders. However, as an adult carer, even though Linda was feeding her mother and helping to wash her, she did not bathe or toilet her out of respect for her mother's pride and dignity. As an adult carer Linda was afforded the satisfaction of being able to act upon this respect:

> I never bathed her. I washed her but my mum did not want me to bath her anyway because obviously she'd got her pride and she hated relying on anybody, so that was very hard for her, so when it got to the stage where she could not even get out of the bath herself, we had the nurse come in for that.

In terms of the other adult carers, both Miriam and Sally also had access to nursing support. Gary had said that the family could cope and had turned down any offers of help.

Conclusion

Young carers are often forced into undertaking intimate caring responsibilities that are both distressing and unappealing to them, as well as to the care receiver. In terms of certain personal tasks, the young carers acquiesce purely on a pragmatic basis. On the other hand, adult carers enjoy increased access to support which allows them some choice in undertaking specific personal tasks (although clearly there may be times when nursing support may not be available, for example during the night).

In chapter seven we report the comments of the social services professional who assumed that if young carers were happy 'changing their parent's nappy' then such a situation was acceptable. Such a viewpoint can only have been informed by subjective assumption, with little consideration for the young carer's own feelings about intimate task performance. We found no evidence of young carers being 'at ease' with their personal, intimate caring role.

Clearly if young carers are to be adequately provided for, then they must be prevented from being coerced into unacceptable caring roles or socialised into roles that they have come to accept, simply because there is no alternative.

Box Two

Caring Responsibilities and Children's Rights

The 1989 UN Convention on the Rights of the Child states that children have the right to develop through play, education and health care and the opportunity to share in social, economic, religious and the political life of the culture. However, for young carers many of these rights are denied them purely through the constraints on their time imposed by the performance of caring tasks and duties.

Regardless of the protection or liberation argument which surrounds the issue of young caring, it is clear that children should not be put at physical risk through lifting their disabled parent/s. In 1948 the Universal Declaration of Human Rights stated that it was the right of all human beings to live out their lives in freedom from fear and want, including the right to health and well being. Children must also qualify for this right and by implication they should not be put at risk by carrying their loved ones.

If young carers intend to continue caring for their parents, then they must be offered alternative forms of support in relation to their (potentially harmful) physical tasks, or when appropriate they must be trained to perform such tasks safely. Professionals must not persist in ignoring the obvious signs of physical strain among young carers.

Networks of Informal and Formal Support for Young Carers

4

Introduction

From talking with the young and adult carers it was clear that support networks fell into two distinct categories: 'informal' or unpaid support provided by immediate family, extended family, neighbours and friends, and 'formal' or paid support represented by professionals such as social workers, GPs, community care assistants, nurses etc. Notably both networks were 'client-based' ie focused on supporting the care *receiver* as opposed to the care giver or provider. Also, formal support was more likely to be made available to those families where primary care was provided by an adult.

One could imagine that informal support would be more specifically oriented towards the nurture and comfort of young carers, but this was not obviously the case. In those families where young carers were providing primary care for a parent/relative in the home, they generally struggled alone with their responsibilities.

In this chapter we will examine not only the degree and types of informal and formal support available to young carers, but also the approach of professionals when confronted with young carers in the family setting.

Even where some form of informal or formal support was available to the care receiver, it was clear that young carers were providing care almost 24 hours a day (as we have already highlighted, even when they were at school many young carers planned the care of their parent, or took time off school to care) and even the assistance of others could not rid them of specific anxieties, for example, the stresses placed on young carers during the night when outside support

was not available, or could not be afforded. Both Jas and Jimmy had interrupted sleep patterns because they lay awake at night listening for signs of distress from their respective parents - 'He'd be in the next room to me. I'd keep thinking to myself is he still breathing? Is he going to have a fit, is he having a fit? It was really worrying' (Jimmy).

All forms of formal support were specifically targeted to meet the needs of the care receiver. We did not find any evidence of professional support aimed expressly at the young carers and no professional had been involved in any discussion with young carers about their needs or their caring roles. Indeed it seemed, as Miriam suggested, that no one really cared about the carer:

> *Nobody seems to care what other people have to put up with - what they have to go through - they don't give a thought for the person who stays behind and looks after the sick person.*

Informal Support - Family Members

Although it would be reasonable to assume that the best and most effective form of support for a young carer would come from other family members, it would seem that this is not the case.

The evidence suggests that even when there are other family members in the house who could help, primary caring responsibilities tend to fall on one child in particular. This child undertakes the main caring role either because he/she cares deeply for the adult and hence feels responsible for their welfare; or cares because of a refined sense of loyalty; or they are 'elected' -

irrespective of their feelings - by other family members (again we can see there are no caring alternatives). This election by other family members can also be instigated by the care receiver's spouse. Out of all the young and adult carers interviewed, five had husbands or fathers who either lived in the house or close by, but who refused to help. We found no evidence of women adults in the house who refused to care.

Even when the young carers' father lived in the family unit and undertook some caring responsibilities, they often refused to do certain tasks. For example, Sarah's father prepared and cooked meals for the family, but the main personal and intimate caring responsibilities fell on Sarah's shoulders, as she said: 'Well dad's got a lot of other things to do'.

The female young carers were noticeably willing to excuse the lack of help from family members, especially their fathers. This was evident in Miriam's case, whose father lived with them, but who had never undertaken any of the caring responsibilities, allowing Miriam to carry out all the caring tasks. His reason for this was that he worked full time. Miriam displayed a remarkable understanding towards her father's attitude, despite his refusal to help and despite her disagreeable relationship with him:

He finds it hard to face, I know because he once said he had lost a wife, he hadn't got a wife who could stand beside him in the pub. He sees other men out with their wives but he wouldn't think of taking her out in the wheelchair.
(Miriam)

Both Diane and Claire's fathers lived close to the family home, but did not offer any caring support. However, neither girls seemed inclined to talk about their relationship with their fathers.

As we have already said, primary caring responsibility seemed to fall on one child's shoulders and this regardless of the number of other siblings living in the family home or close by. Interestingly, where there were girls in the family and where the care receiver was female, caring tasks were always undertaken by one of the daughters. This notion of caring as 'women's work' was reflected in Sarah's attitude, who said of her twin brother: 'Well he can't do it because he's a boy'. However, even Sarah's elder sister did not undertake any caring responsibilities and there seemed to be no age variable involved in young caring. What was clear was that the caring role is determined by coercion or the election of a sometimes less dominant child by other family members. Sarah was elected for the primary caring role by her elder sister, who excused herself because she would often be unavailable for caring duties:

She [sister] doesn't want to help sort of thing. You know she keeps saying 'Oh I've got to go out and phone someone' when I ask her to help me shower mum.
(Sarah)

It was quite striking to witness the amount of responsibility some older siblings would allow the young carer to undertake. For example, Miriam had left school at 16 to care full time for her mother, and yet she received persistent criticism from her older brother and sisters (who did not live in the family home) about her caring abilities. Her sisters were not prepared to make any sacrifices in order to care for their mother and her brother's attitude was determined by gender assumptions (ie that caring is 'women's work'):

> *Paul can't do much because it's a woman and he says if it had been my dad he'd have been the one looking after him and I think oh no you wouldn't because my mother would have done it.*
>   (Miriam)

Not only did the young carers demonstrate a strong level of commitment to their parent/s, but their level of tolerance towards the lack of family help - especially support from their siblings - was also quite remarkable, as was their readiness to justify the behaviour of their brothers and sisters. For example, Jas had suffered many adverse effects from providing primary care for his parents, and from the lack of equity in the division of tasks, and yet he willingly 'made excuses' for his brothers:

> *My younger brother can't help because he sleeps in a lot and my older brother works nights.*

The same was also true of Linda. Her brother worked shifts which she said made it difficult for him to undertake many of the caring duties, even though she also had a full time job. She also seemed to imply that he did not cope as well emotionally with the caring role.

There were some young carers who had to rely on support from their younger brothers and sisters, especially when the young carers themselves were at school. For example Claire had to rely on her 13 year old sister and four year old brother at certain times, and she could not have managed the caring routine as well without their help, but she only called on their support when it was absolutely necessary.

Although the young carers were generally tolerant towards the lack of familial support, often the lack of help also served to drive a rift between family members. In such instances it seemed that the lack of help was considered by those who cared as a sign of indifference as well as an act of betrayal. For example, Jimmy's brother did not offer any help when their father's brain tumour was diagnosed, which served to alienate the brothers: 'When he was told about dad, he just didn't want to know. I can't forgive him for that' (Jimmy).

Grandparents

On the whole it seemed that grandparents did not provide a network of support for young carers either. Out of all the carers interviewed, only Diane relied on help from her grand-parents, who lived just a short drive away. Diane was also the only young carer interviewed whose grandparents provided support for *her* as well as her mother - 'they help partly, but mostly they give me someone to talk to if I need it'.

However, generally grandparents seemed conspicuous by their absence, and yet the young carers tried to rationalise their reluctance to help - once again the familiar tolerance was in evidence. For example, Zia and Mansour's grandparents and other relatives lived in Birmingham and rarely came to visit, even though their support would have been very welcome. The boys rationalised this by saying they lived too far away to be able to lend their support.

It appeared that Alison's grandparents had abandoned her. At the onset of care Alison was a very young child and in great need of familial support, especially as her mother's illness coincided with her father's sudden death. However, help never materialised from her extended family, who lived just eight miles away. Indeed Alison had been left to manage on her own for so long that she eventually rejected any kind of help they offered later:

They did say they were going to help, doing the garden and everything, but that's never happened. I needed help then, but now I just don't want to know.

For others such as Debra, her grand-mother only stepped in to help during crisis points in Debra's life, for example when Debra ran away from home because of her mother's violence towards her.

Neighbours, Friends and Family Pets!
It was clear from the findings that once again, in relation to family friends and neighbours, support was aimed specifically at the care receiver. Furthermore such friends only seemed to become involved during times of crisis or difficulty, and sometimes then only by accident.

For example, Alison's neighbours only

came to her mother's aid when she fell and Alison did not know how to cope. She was forced to go to her immediate neighbours for help. Only then did they discover (after several years of living next door to one another) that their neighbour was a nurse at the local hospital.

Diane's neighbours also helped during a crisis, but only at this time, and it was only through a family pet that they intervened to lend their support:

My mother was going out to the dustbin and she slipped and fell and she smacked her head on the concrete and knocked herself out. Next door's have got a cat and he found my mum and he went in and was meowing like crazy and they came out to find my mum on the floor. The cat's only got three legs anyway and he spends a lot of his time round here.
  (Diane)

The findings certainly did not reveal a community support network of neighbours and friends which the young carers could call on for help. Out of all the young and adult carers interviewed, only Claire had access to a network of neighbourly support. But again neighbours only came in during difficult times, when Claire and her brother and sister were simply unable to care. The type of support offered by these neighbours was akin to a 'sitting service'. We did not find any evidence of friends or neighbours undertaking any caring responsibilities other than 'keeping an eye on' the care receiver, or sitting with them while the young carer was out.

Such a lack of community support could be explained by the transience of residency, the fragmentation of the community (the erosion of primary groupings) or indeed the Thatcher sentiment that there is no longer such a thing as society, only individuals and their families. But it may be that people are reluctant to involve themselves with families in need because the boundaries of commitment are uncertain (ie they are unsure of the level and duration of commitment they may have to give). It could! also be due to the fear of, or inability to deal with, illness and disability.

However, whatever the explanation, we found little evidence of a so-called community spirit. Indeed, four of the young carers had experienced open hostility from the local community. For example, Debra was often taunted when she went out with her mother, especially as her mother's behaviour was unpredictable at times due to the effects of her illness. Debra said she was also regularly teased because her mother didn't dress her 'properly': 'People round here, they are always picking on people if you've got anything wrong with your mum'. This was clearly very distressing for Debra, and during the interview she often returned to the fact that her attire made her open to mockery. Alderson (1992:166) reminds us that for children 'normality' is very important, such as dressing like their friends and being able to do the same things and that there is 'pain and loneliness' in being different.

Sarah also experienced what we might call 'community abuse' because she said her family was different from other families in the neighbourhood:

Like a new family moving into the estate, they want to get to know you and stuff like that, but we didn't get along with people so they started smashing windows and stuff like that.

Carers Groups and Voluntary Support

Out of all those interviewed Miriam was the only carer who had attended a carers group as well as a group for the carers of multiple sclerosis sufferers. At this point Miriam was still at school and found the experience quite alienating:

The four of us went one week and didn't like it and never went back. We didn't think it was for us because we were only kids and everybody else were grown ups. Everyone else was an adult, like it was a husband looking after a wife, or a wife looking after a husband. It wasn't anybody's children looking after a parent.

Even as an adult, Miriam still felt ostracised when she attended a carers group at the local day centre. She went once, but 'because it was all parents again, looking after children, and there were no children looking after parents, I just thought this is not for me'.

Clearly, it is important to recognise both children who care and the nature of the caring relationship when planning voluntary support for carers. However, the idea of young carers support groups as a concept and potential source of help, was not well received by the young carers during interview. Many of the young carers had never spoken about their caring role before, and it appeared that many of them would also feel unwilling to talk about their experiences in front of others. As Jimmy said, even if group support had been offered, he would not have attended:

> Me, no way. I personally would not have sat in a room say with 15 other people chatting away to everyone. I wouldn't have done that at all.

Fear was clearly a major consideration - fear of calling attention to their situation, and fear of the consequences of outside intervention in their lives. Pride was also a significant issue - most of the young carers were reluctant to let anyone know their circumstances. Linda commented:

> I suppose in a way you want to keep it as quiet as possible. You don't want anybody else to know about it. And I suppose I would have found it very difficult in a group like that with a lot of carers. So it was easier just to keep it in the family.

The only other form of voluntary support evident was the support provided by local vicars and religious leaders, but again this was aimed specifically at the care receiver and not young carers. However, as a number of referrals (at the identification stage) came from vicars, it was clear that they were at least identifying young carers in families.

Formal Support

Once again it was clear that professional support was aimed specifically at the care receiver rather than young carers. Out of all those interviewed, only Claire had received

medical attention through communication links between her mother's community nurse and Claire's GP.

Not one professional individual or agency had engaged the young carers in any discussion about their caring responsibilities, experiences or needs. This seems to be a glaring omission, especially considering the overwhelming response by young carers that they would like to talk to someone about their caring roles (see chapter six). Indeed, as Twigg *et al* (1990:5) suggested: 'Carers are rarely themselves the focus of an intervention'. If we replace 'carers' with *young* carers, then we may say they are *never* the focus of an intervention.

In some cases professionals were indirectly involved with young carers because of familial problems. For example, Sarah was assigned a social worker because her father refused to send her to school. But the social worker did not discuss Sarah's caring responsibilities with her. However, the majority of external formal intervention came in the form of 'home helps' (as the young carers called them), but who are now known as Community Care Assistants (CCAs).

Community Care Assistance

It was often difficult to establish the various support networks actually involved in the families because the young carers could not always be precise about the types of help supporting the care receivers.

However, CCAs seemed to have the most input into families and seemed to perform a variety of tasks from bathing and showering the care receiver, to tidying the house and basic domestic duties. However, it was clear that the adult carers seemed to enjoy increased access to professional support and could also more readily distinguish between types of support available. All the adult carers had been offered CCA support at some time, but only five out of the 11 young carers' parents received community care assistance.

From the young carers' perspective CCAs appeared to be 'shadowy' domestic figures who had little or no contact or involvement with them. On the other hand it appeared that adult carers enjoyed a better relationship with the CCAsand nursing support. For example, Miriam said that it was only when she became an 'adult' that the nurse engaged her in conversation:

> They didn't talk to me when I was younger, but they do now. We never really used to see them - only if mum had a sore leg or something, they used to do the dressing and leave, that was it.

This could be because as the carers achieved adult status their fear of outside intervention diminished. Thus adult carers were able to enjoy a greater freedom in their relationship with these professionals. However, as we have already seen, such profess-ionals were not involving the *young* carers at all in any discussion about their roles, thus maintaining and reinforcing the veil of silence surrounding the young caring experience.

It was clear that both Linda and Miriam were very grateful for CCA and nursing support, and seemed to enjoy greater levels of communication and interaction with them. However, it was evident that even adult carers were not approaching such

professionals for their own needs. They may have been more willing to discuss the care receiver's needs and feelings, but adult carers did not communicate their own requirements and anxieties to these professionals.

The CCA's tasks appeared to vary enormously - their working schedules beset with inconsistencies. Recent guidance on implementing the NHS and Community Care Act 1990 suggests that services should be provided 'within available resources.' Clearly then local authority decisions about CCA support are going to vary considerably as there is no national consensus on provision. As Doyle and Harding (1992:71) point out: 'There are wide variations in the availability of services between authorities. For example, someone who would qualify for a home help in one area would not in another.'

From a local perspective, this inconsistency was confirmed by social services who, at the time of the study, were in the process of drawing up guidelines on community care assistance, emphasising the distinctions between the tasks of CCA's and nursing support, as well as the particular duties relating to both. There had been some acknowledgement of the wide variations relating to these issues across districts.

Interestingly, although the professionals involved in the young carers' families did not communicate with the young carers, the duties the CCA's performed and the point at which they withdrew their support seemed very much determined by the ability and age of the young carers.

Young carers reported that CCA support was being withdrawn when the child/ren were considered a 'suitable' age to undertake the caring responsibilities themselves. However, definitions about 'suitable' ages varied considerably. Furthermore, professionals had denied or did not believe such an informal policy was in operation. During interview a carers development worker said: 'I've heard people say their home help has told them they are not caring anymore because the daughter is old enough to care, but I can't believe it'.

However, this was undoubtedly the case, as Sarah, Alison, Zia and Mansour all confirmed that CCA support had been withdrawn or threatened to be withdrawn when they reached a particular age, which varied from 12 - 16 years in each case. Further investigation among professionals in social services found that the imposition of such criteria was not recognised, nor was it official 'policy', but because the area was so large, such inconsistencies and street-level policies were inevitable.

It was also clear that much rested on the individual personality of the CCA/nurse in terms of the nature and extent of their support:

> My mum had this sort of rash on her bum and it really hurt and they came to deal with it, put a plaster and some stuff on it and mum asked if she could give her a shower and she told her there was no point in her coming if she had two daughters who could help. They said we only come to the people who need our help.
>
> (Sarah)

Clearly the withdrawal of support has

considerable implications for the level and nature of responsibilities that fall on the young carers shoulders. Often the young carers seemed to feel that the support they were providing was superior to the support offered by the CCA or community nurse. For example, Jimmy argued that he was far more useful as an untrained informal carer than his father's CCA:

> She couldn't do anything. She didn't know what to do, she just used to come and sit down and make sure everything was all right with him. I was doing more good than what she was doing.

Perhaps in this case, community care assistance was not the most suitable form of outside support. Jimmy's father was very ill and clearly needed full nursing support. The CCA should have communicated this need to the community nursing division.

Social Workers

Four of the young carers interviewed had been assigned a social worker, but only one of them was seeing their social worker around the time of interview. From young carers' statements, it was clear that these professionals only intervened at crisis points, or when the law had been broken. For example, Jimmy and Sarah had been assigned social workers because of their failure to attend school.

Debra's social worker was brought in because she ran away from her mother in the middle of the night and had rung the police for help. Claire had also been visited by a social worker in the past, but she hadn't seen her for some considerable time and she refused to say why the social worker had intervened.

At no time did the social workers talk to the young carers about their caring roles. They might have been brought in because of the effects of caring (ie lack of school attendance, crises) but there was a tendency to treat the effect rather than the cause. In all the cases the relationship between the young carers and the social workers was far from satisfactory. From the young carers' perspectives, attitudes to social workers ranged from indifference (Sarah) to dislike (Jimmy) and rejection (Claire - 'I told her to fuck off, I haven't seen her since').

Although it is clear that social workers have acquired a somewhat derogatory image over recent years - which to some extent has been perpetrated and reinforced by the media - it is perhaps understandable that young carers should identify with this image as well as create their own aversion (based on fear) to any 'authority figure' who could potentially threaten the pattern of their lives.

However, this fear may not be unfounded, as Meredith (1991a:9) points out: 'At present people often fear that a social worker's response will be to put their child into care and sadly it is apparent that the option of care proceedings is used, or threatened, much too early'.

This may have been true in Claire's case, for although she would not be specific about social work involvement, it seemed that there may have been some concern over her ability to look after her mother:

I don't like social workers. I can cope.

I've told my mum I'll always be there.
   (Claire)

In Sarah's case she seemed to be the unfortunate victim caught in the middle of 'warring' agencies. Sarah's father had been prosecuted for refusing to send Sarah to school, and she was assigned a social worker. At the time of interview Sarah said she hadn't seen her social worker for over two years ('She has more holidays than anyone I know'). However, Sarah was clearly in urgent need of attention. She could not read or write but was desperate to learn, and she was also clearly suffering some emotional difficulties due to her abuse by 'several boys' outside school one night two years previously. Sarah no longer went out of the house and part of her reluctance to go to school was her association with the attack.

Sarah's was a complex case, but it was Sarah who was suffering most as she was caught in the middle of cross-agency intervention both from the education authorities and social services, neither of whom were focusing on Sarah's direct needs. Sarah had decided that her social worker 'didn't care anymore'.

Both Jimmy and Debra were assigned social workers during crisis points in their lives. However, even though the workers intervened when perhaps the children most needed support, neither Jimmy or Debra wanted the kind of help that was offered.

For example, Debra ran away from her mother because her mother had become violent towards her and she desperately wanted to leave, but social services tried to reunite her with her mother on several occasions. Although the aim (ie to keep the two together) was apparently based on good intention, the reality was that Debra was placed at considerable risk. The social worker's initial response when Debra first ran away was to improve their living conditions by securing a bungalow for Debra and her mother:

> They were trying to get a scheme working to say well we've done it, we've done this and it's working and everything, and it was never working all the time.
> (Debra)

Debra felt that social services wanted to appear to be doing the 'right thing', but she said they never listened to her and never acted in her best interests, 'I was always ignored', she said. Even when she was a young girl caring for her mother she could sense she was being patronised:

> It's another thing that makes me really mad. When somebody goes in and sits (and I'm not referring to you) and talks to me, like there is social workers coming in sitting and talking to me and they have not been through it and they sit there and they patronise me, like I will sit there and they will ask me questions and everything and talk to me like I'm a kid - at that point I wasn't a child because I was doing exactly the same things as they were at home, you know what I mean, like when they went home they was putting the dinner on and I was and they made me really mad because they used to talk to me like I was a child and I used to feel like

> getting up and saying 'don't talk to me like that!'
> (Debra)

Such attitudes are perhaps due to a lack of understanding about children's ability to comprehend their situation or know what is best for them. This certainly seemed to be true from the evidence of a further example in Debra's history. Debra was referred to a social worker at a later crisis point in her life, by a Huntington's Chorea support worker. Debra's educational ability had clearly been severely affected by her lack of school attendance, but she was more than capable of understanding what her needs were, as well as those of her mother. However, the social worker failed to perceive this and conducted the interview with Debra somewhat insensitively:

> The social worker told me she wouldn't believe what I told her about myself or my mum because the Huntington's Chorea woman had told her I was a...'habitual liar', is that how you say it?
> (Debra)

This phrase was clearly not part of Debra's vocabulary, but she remembered it all too well. It was clear that the interview and what the social worker had said to Debra, only served to undermine what little trust Debra may have had in such professionals.

Jimmy on the other hand seemed to suffer from the inconsistencies between the different social workers involved in his case. It is likely that young carers could, over time, be assigned various social workers (social workers move on, departments are reorganised, young carers move home) and such a situation certainly does not facilitate the development of a good and trusting relationship between client and professional. However, this is what Jimmy needed most of all - someone to trust; someone to talk to.

As we have already highlighted, Jimmy was assigned a social worker because of his lack of school attendance (because he was looking after his father 24 hours a day). However, once again the professional response was to treat the symptom and not the cause:

When they did find out I was looking after him and that he had a brain tumour, social workers didn't really do much about it. Then I was taken to court and threatened to be put into care.
(Jimmy)

This reaction exacerbated Jimmy's distrust and fear of social workers. He desperately wanted to stay with his father and was afraid the authorities would separate them.

All the time they were involved in Jimmy's case, no social worker or any professional ever spoke to Jimmy about his caring role or his feelings about caring. Again, there was no examination of anything beyond the immediate problem:

The social workers...they were terrible. I should have hit one of them but I didn't. I mean they were nasty and the answer to us was 'put him in care, put your dad in hospital, best thing you can do'.
(Jimmy)

When Jimmy's father was eventually admitted to hospital just before he died, a social worker broke the news to Jimmy about his father's terminal condition:

She just said 'your dad's going to die'. Oh thanks for telling me - and that was it, she give me a lift home [where he was alone] and that was it.
(Jimmy)

Like all our young carers, Jimmy's was undoubtedly a complex case. He was determined to stay with his father and yet caring for him alone and under such extreme circumstances was clearly detrimental to his well-being. The effects of having to watch his father die, and living as they were without money or outside support, were manifold. Jimmy willingly admitted that his personality underwent some dramatic changes during the time he was caring, and he said he became 'an unpleasant person' for a while.

In addition to these anxieties, Jimmy was being constantly threatened with care orders. He was also at the mercy of inter-agency disagreements concerning his case. Jimmy was eventually given a Guardian Ad Litem, and a court case ensued. Jimmy's social worker spoke on Jimmy's behalf, opposing the Guardian's recommendations:

My Guardian Ad Litem was the most vicious person I've ever met. In court she stood up and said 'I think Jimmy would be best off in care - we'll put him in a secure home' I've never done a thing wrong in my life - never done anything violent.

  (Jimmy)

It was Jimmy's social worker who suggested he should stay at home. Clearly the inconsistencies here caused Jimmy some considerable distress and confusion. Jimmy was put on probation for eight months and was told if he didn't go to school in that time he would be put into care. Jimmy's father was very ill by this stage and needed constant attention and Jimmy would not leave him. He even barricaded the house door, so no one could take him away.

General Practitioners - Delivering Bad News

Twigg (1992:70) has argued that general practitioners (GPs) are ideally placed to recognise the needs of carers as the majority of the population contact a doctor at some time. However, they stress that 'carers have to be very assertive and self-confident to shift attention to their needs' (p 72).

It was clear from our interviews that GP's are not recognising the needs of young carers, but at the same time the young carers are not assertive enough, nor necessarily willing and confident to approach GPs in terms of their own needs.

We found no evidence of young carers approaching the family doctor for support or treatment for care-related problems. During the interviews GPs were discussed only in terms of the care receiver's needs, and at no point had doctors involved the young carers in discussions about the care receiver's diagnosis, treatment or the management of care.

It has been argued that GPs do vary in their responses, particularly in relation to social issues in which they have little training (see Twigg 1992:70-4). However, two issues which would improve relations between GPs and young carers ie accessibility and flexibility, are undermined through the constraints on practice time.

For example, although Gary respected and liked the family doctor he realised he could not discuss his caring problems with him. At one time Gary was concerned about some of his brother's behavioural problems, which he did not know how to deal with. However, he knew his doctor would not have the time to talk to him about this problem:

I can only see my doctor for ten minutes, so in ten minutes I can't really talk about what we need to talk about because it takes up a lot of time, but from what I can gather, it's the same with all doctors these days.

  (Gary)

Such time constraints coupled with the nature of practice (ie in the consulting room under pressure) result in insensitive management especially it seems in relation to delivering bad news. The way such news was delivered had a lasting effect on those young carers whose parents had terminal conditions.

Linda commented:

The doctor who told my mum she was terminal, he was awful to her. She was in this room and he said 'right, that's it, get your house in order. Go home and get your life in order' and he sent her out the room. She felt suicidal.

Jimmy's father had a similar experience, but he was told the bad news with Jimmy at his side:

They said 'we are sorry to tell you but you've got another brain tumour and we can't do anything about it, you've got two weeks to live. Make arrangements'. And I was standing there. That's all they said 'you've got two weeks to live'. I lost my rag and dad just...he just took it. I don't know how he could.
    (Jimmy)

Furthermore, when Jimmy's father died, the hospital did not tell Jimmy immediately and when he asked to see his father they refused. While Jimmy was waiting, he saw his father's body being wheeled to the mortuary.

It seems that GPs are equally guilty of treating the symptom rather than the cause. For example, Claire said during her second interview that 'things had been getting on top of her' and she had been to her GP with stress symptoms. The GP prescribed tranquillisers. This approach reinforces the notion that 'the traditional bias in medicine towards a narrow focus on the patient - and sometimes only on the conditions - reinforces this tendency. General Practitioners tend to define the problem first in medical terms and secondly in terms of the individual patient' (Twigg 1992:72).

In terms of the provision of information GP's might be ideally placed in this respect, but they are not using this pivotal position to the advantage of young carers. In chapter six we will discuss further the information needs of young carers and the ability of such professionals to supply such information.

Conclusion

The only professionals involved in young carers' families were community care assistants, nurses, social workers and general practitioners. Furthermore, the level of their involvement and the nature and extent of their duties varied enormously.

At no point did any of these professionals engage the young carers in discussions about their caring roles or experiences, and only social work support focused specifically on individual young carers.

As we have seen there were inconsistencies in the application and withdrawal of CCA provision. Clearly the nature and extent of CCA involvement depends on the specific requirements of individual clients. Thus flexibility is a prerequisite of CCA and community nursing provision, but such flexibility must also extend to the identification of young carers in families as well as provision for their needs.

Social workers have further obstacles to overcome if they are to gain the trust and respect of young carers. They must withstand the negative effects of media attention as well as young carers' fears that social workers 'put children into care'. Often, the outcome of social work intervention is at variance with the needs and wishes of young carers.

General practitioners must also identify and acknowledge the reality of young caring. Presently, GPs are not identifying or supporting young carers, nor are they

mediators in the provision of information,
despite their central locus in the community,
their access to vast numbers of the
population and their pivotal position in the
brave new world of community care.

Professionals entering such families need
to identify both the client as well as the carer's
needs, especially where the carer is a child.
Even if individual professionals cannot
personally administer appropriate support,
they must recognise familial and carer
requirements and involve other agencies,
with the necessary consultation between
young carers and their families.

The Effects of Caring - The Best of Times and the Worst of Times

5

Introduction

It is clear that there are developmental and emotional implications in the long term effects of caring on children. A child who is prevented from engaging fully in play, education and social interaction is arguably going to suffer adverse effects in early or later life.

We have already examined the physical effects of caring, for example interrupted sleep patterns and physical injury through lifting. In this chapter we will examine the effects of caring on children in terms of their silence, friendships, social life and education, as well as the effects on their personal and professional ambitions.

In terms of emotional effects, we will discuss their memories, crises, grief and happiness or what we have termed 'the best of times and the worst of times'. We will also focus on the effects on the caring relationship, between care provider and care receiver.

Although we cannot sufficiently gauge the long term effects of caring on a child, previous research has highlighted the problems associated with young caring and the effects on children's personal and educational development. As Meredith (1991a:9) points out: 'There is also evidence of more complex stresses; personal, social and educational development can be affected by missing school, or the lack of opportunity to sustain friendships or participate in activities; and these problems continue into later life'.

Furthermore, if it is true that the provision of services can reduce levels of stress on carers (Twigg, Atkin and Perring, 1990:1-14), then presently there are no methods of reducing the strain on *young*

carers as there are no services currently targeted at their needs.

As legislation on children's rights has more than adequately highlighted their prerogatives (the 1969 Family Law Reform Act, the 1989 UN Convention on the Rights of the Child, the 1989 Children Act) it seems remarkable that society continues to perpetuate the neglect of children who care.

Alderson (1992:157) has drawn attention to the argument that children should not take over from their parents - in a sense become the guardians of their own parents - under the age of 16. These young carers however are to some extent both guardians of their own welfare and, as we have already indicated, their own parents' parent.

The Silent Carers - Talking to Someone

It emerged that one of the effects of caring on young carers was their inability or reluctance to talk about their conditions and experiences. In effect, caring had served to silence them. The young carers were often unable to tell anyone about their caring circumstances for several reasons: because they found it difficult to talk about; they didn't want anyone else to know and so kept it within the family; or they were afraid of the consequences of telling.

Very few of the young carers interviewed had told anyone about their caring situation, mainly for the above reasons.

However, considering the relative ease with which many of them talked during interview, it was clear that very few people had ever asked them or encouraged them to talk about their experiences and their needs. In short, their self-imposed silence was reinforced by the disinterest of others.

It is important to note that when we discussed who the young carers had discussed their experiences or circumstances with, they only responded in terms of telling friends or other school children. At no point did they reveal they had taken professionals into their confidence.

Out of all the young carers interviewed, only Diane found it easy to talk about her caring responsibilities with her friends at school. The other young carers wanted to limit the amount of people who knew about their situation to family members and possible supporters. Much of this reluctance had its roots in pride, for example, Claire said:

I didn't used to talk about it. I didn't want anybody knowing our business. I still don't but I've grown up a lot, I've had to. You've got to.

Both Miriam and Alison were afraid that knowledge of their caring circumstances would induce ridicule from outsiders:

I thought people would just laugh at me.
(Miriam)

Or Alison:

You know at school they're all two faced and God knows what they're all saying and so you just keep it to yourself.

For some, such as Linda, even talking about her caring role within the family was very difficult:
You skirt round the problem and don't

want to bring it up. Because it is happening and on-going and obviously a very frightening thing you are going through as well you try to block it out and don't really want to talk about it.

These young carers need encouragement to talk about their experiences and needs. As we have already indicated, many of the young carers were talking for the first time about their caring routines when they participated in the interviews, and yet for many it was a cathartic experience. For example, one young carer agreed to participate in the research because she had heard of someone else who had been interviewed and who had found the process 'really helpful'. Young carers' self-inflicted silence (maintained through fear and a heightened sense of pride) is no reason for the persistent neglect of their needs.

Social Life, Friendships and the 'Caring Curfew'

Friendships and socialising were among the top five most commonly discussed topics among the young carers. The findings revealed that in relation to both topics, proximity to the caring environment was a key factor in the nature and extent of the young carers' friendships and social activities.

The young carers lives were very much caught up in their immediate environment, ie they conducted their friendships and social lives within close proximity to the family home. Indeed, many of the young carers interpreted 'socialising' as a visit to a friend's house (always close by) and not as a night at a disco or the pictures etc.

The pressure of their caring responsibilities had a significant impact on the nature and extent of their social activities. For example, when Claire was asked if she went out, she said she only went to her 'mates across the road', or, the friend she used to have 'lives in Radford now, so I don't see her' - even though Radford was only two or three miles from her home. Claire's life was very much home-centred - the boundaries to her life were the family home and the immediate neighbourhood (ie the street where she lived).

Four other factors also significantly affected the young carers' social activities: the pressure of their caring duties; the attitude of the care receiver (who didn't like or want the carer to go out); emotional pressures such as the young carers' feelings of guilt and loyalty; and their friends' attitudes towards their caring responsibilities. In certain cases, all these factors combined. This was certainly true for Miriam who, when she was younger, couldn't stay out late because of the demands of caring, thus her friends started to neglect her (they didn't invite her out because they knew she often couldn't go). Miriam also felt guilty when she did go out, and her mother didn't like her socialising away from the family home anyway and often used to cause Miriam more work if she stayed out 'too long':

I went out a couple of times once and stayed out a bit later than I normally did, come home and she's messed herself. I came in a happy mood, had a few drinks with my friends and then I've got to start stripping the bed and things like that...then I felt guilty, when I realised

one day what I was doing, I thought I shouldn't go out so much.
(Miriam)

At the time of interview Miriam had stopped socialising and only ever went out to visit her friend locally. Also, the demands of full time caring meant that Miriam didn't make any new friends, her only social contacts were with her family and the community care assistant.

If the young carers did go out, they were often the victims of what we have termed the 'caring curfew', in that they always had to be home by a certain time. Linda, Jas, Alison and Diane all said if they went out they had to be home early, either because of the demands of their caring duties, they were anxious about leaving their parent/s, or because the care receiver insisted on it.

Even though many of the young carers were clearly dissatisfied with the restrictions caring imposed on their social lives, they did seem to adjust over time and always organised their priorities in favour of the welfare of their parent/s. However, some of them initially fought against these restrictions by lying about their social activities. For example, Alison spent a considerable time rebelling against the restrictions imposed on her by her caring duties, especially as she felt she was being 'left out' by her friends:

All my friends were going out, you know and I had to stop in and do the ironing and like I just rebelled against every-thing. I couldn't go out when I wanted to go out but my mum needed the things doing there and then and I didn't want to do it there and then.

Jas had even lied to his father in order to stop out a little longer in the evenings. Previously he had brought his friends back to the house, but as his father's condition worsened and he tried to drive Jas's friends out of the house, so Jas was forced to lie to his father about his whereabouts. Often his mother also used to lie for him:

> *I don't stop out long because he doesn't like it, but my mum doesn't tell him I go out at all. He gets worried so much, mum lets him think I'm upstairs.*
> (Jas)

Some of the young carers such as Sarah, Debra and Manoj, were totally isolated in that they had no friends, and remained in the family home most of the time. However, other factors also influenced their lack of social activity. As we have already seen, Debra's mother did not dress her 'properly' and she was ridiculed by the neighbours. Sarah's neighbours were also antagonistic and she didn't like going far because she was afraid (since she'd been attacked outside school). Manoj said he stayed in the house because he had no friends.

However, another major factor affecting the young and adult carers' social lives was that often their friends didn't fully appreciate the time they had to spend on caring, because they had no understanding of the caring experience. Some of the carers said they thought their friends lacked the maturity to understand the nature of the caring role:

> *Some of them at school they're just like*

kids and act like it a lot of the time...but we've got more experience of life.
(Mansour)

Jimmy lost his friends once his father became ill because of their inability to understand his situation:

> *They still used to come round, but they couldn't do a thing and didn't know what to say, didn't know what to do. I couldn't talk to them about it. As I see it one was too young to understand and the other one was too stupid to understand.*
> (Jimmy)

It seemed it was only those friends who had been through similar experiences who could understand the young carers' circumstances. Out of all those interviewed only Linda had a friend who understood what she was going through because her mother had also suffered from cancer. However, Linda's other friends were less sympathetic:

> *My other two friends, although they were sympathetic sometimes if they wanted me to come out with them they couldn't really understand if I said 'well look I can't, I have got this responsibility. I have got to look after my mum, she's on her own and I can't leave her'.*

In responding to the various pressures of caring, young carers are missing out on social opportunities which themselves decline as caring continues over time. In doing so, they are also missing out on a much needed break from their caring responsibilities.

However, over time some of the young carers managed to adapt their friendships to accommodate their caring responsibilities. So much so that if a newly made friend couldn't adapt to the caring routine then they did not remain friends. As Alison said: 'if they don't fit in, then they're out'. Gary had also adopted this attitude towards his friends. However, it takes courage and strength as well as an acceptance of the caring role in order to maintain such an approach to friendships, and many of the young carers had not yet reached this stage.

Not one of the young or adult carers enjoyed a regular social life nor had access to friendship networks. Both groups , at some point, had been adversely affected by the caring process.

Effects on School Life

Ten out of the 14 carers interviewed (excluding Caroline) had missed school at some time because of the demands of caring, and some of them had missed a considerable amount of school.

Although it is clearly a fundamental right of all children to have access to education, some of the young carers were being denied this right because they had no choice but to take time off school to care. Some of the young carers were also experiencing difficulties at school, not necessarily because of their caring responsibilities, but there was some correlation because of the indirect pressures of caring.

For example, Jas had been expelled from school for violence against a teacher (although he vehemently denied his guilt during interview). However, Jas was undertaking primary caring responsibilities for both his parents at home and often lost sleep at night because his father needed 24 hour attention. He had also run away several times because of the pressures on him at home. No one at school had investigated Jas's home life. No one had discussed nor indeed identified his caring circumstances. It was clear that Jas needed support from his teachers and some degree of consultation. His expulsion from school only served to exacerbate his stress. Again we can see the focus on the symptom rather than the cause.

The Sandwell research (Page, 1988:31-6) aimed to determine the extent of caring among school children, and identified various problems associated with caring and its effects on school life: poor concentration, difficulties in doing homework, poor attendance, lateness and lack of parental support. The recommendations included more flexible approaches for young carers in school, more emotional support, counselling and support networks, as well as training among pastoral staff and collaboration between teachers, EWO's and other agencies. These recommendations would undoubtedly be effective in terms of adequate provision for and recognition of young carers in school. However, we found no evidence that any such principles were being observed.

The evidence highlighted two ways in which young carers were coming to the attention of teaching and school staff: children were forced to explain their continual absences or lateness, and they had to explain their parents' absence from parents' evening.

Often teaching staff came across young

carers by accident. However, once such a discovery had been made, generally little further action was taken. For example, Miriam's teacher had discovered she was caring for her mother because her mother did not attend parents' evening (even though Miriam had missed a great deal of school, and an exam, because of her caring responsibilities at home). The teacher's response was both unsatisfactory and embarrassing for Miriam:

> *The teacher asked me who did the cleaning up in the house and I said that I did it and she asked me if I wanted to have some of my class mates to come round and help me clean up. I said no thank you. Then she bought my mother a plant. She got the class to club together and bought my mother a plant!*

Often the young carers were forced to explain their absences or lateness to teachers in front of the whole class. Even more surprising was the fact that when the teachers found out, they often either ignored the problem or were antagonistic or disbelieving toward the young carer. Manoj, Jas, Debra and Sarah all said that once they had explained their circumstances to their teachers, they either accepted it, were mistrustful or dismissed the problem. Debra said: 'No one ever really bothered about me at school'. Sarah told us her teacher had said: 'As long as you're not off too long, because you've got your education to consider'. Sarah added: 'But I've been off school over two year now'.

It seems remarkable that teaching staff consistently failed to intervene or offer their support to these young carers. At no time did any of the teachers act on the statements from the young carers, in fact they were either indifferent or disbelieving in their responses to these children. Both Manoj and Jas's absences were allowed to continue unchecked. In Debra's case, her teachers clearly did not believe her explanation, as the following story reveals:

> *When I was at school most of the teachers thought I was playing on it and that like every time I was late I'd say 'I'm sorry I had to take care of my mum' and it was like 'don't give me that' and once Mrs [ ] was really nasty, and I wasn't looking for sympathy. I was just looking for someone to understand what I had to do. I wasn't like every other kid, I didn't just have to get up and just eat my cornflakes and then go to school. She came in one day and said 'I'm sick and tired of you looking for sympathy and everything'. I said 'I am not looking for sympathy'. I said 'have you got a mum and dad?' and she said yes. 'Have you got grandparents, got lots of cousins and uncles and aunties and everything?' and she said yes. I said 'well good for you, I've barely got a mum who I'm trying to look after and I haven't got a dad to back me up' and I was shouting and saying 'I'm trying to get by as best I can and without your support how am I supposed to get on well in school?' She turned round and said 'Oh well then we'll let this one pass by'.*
> (Debra)

Even when Debra was very young no one

believed that she was having to care for her mother, but she reasoned that 'no one would believe a nine year old kid anyway'.

As we have already mentioned, school parents' evening was often when teaching staff identified young carers - evidence again of the tendency of professionals to focus on the adult perspective: it was only when parents had to be accountable, had to be visible at school that questions were asked.

For example, Diane didn't miss school unless her mother's condition deteriorated, or she had an illness additional to the MS. However, Diane's mother couldn't go to parents' evening unless wheelchair access was organised. Once Diane's teachers discovered she was caring for her mother, they acted immediately, but only in relation to her mother's attendance at parent's evening. No further support was offered:

They were really helpful because the lift was actually in the school canteen which was locked after school hours so they had to get the keys and open up all the canteen and the doors to get mum in.
(Diane)

Four of the young carers interviewed had experienced serious problems at school or had taken long-term absences, at which point the school authorities usually intervened. Arguably it is at this point when support could be offered to the young carers and their families and flexible arrangements made to prevent the onset of further problems. However, the general response was to prosecute. Jimmy and his father were both prosecuted for Jimmy's lack of attendance at

school, as was Sarah's father.

Jimmy was absent from school for two years while looking after his father. He wouldn't go to school because he was afraid his father would have a fit and hurt himself while Jimmy was away:

If I'd have gone to school he would have tried to get up the stairs and one time he had a fit, he came tumbling down the stairs head first and cracked his skull open where he had his brain tumour. I was standing there. I'd never seen a fit before. He was hanging there biting his tongue, snapped his glasses, smacked me one. He was hanging right out there on the banister about to drop off there and that was the worst thing.

The education authorities investigated Jimmy's case and took his father to court. Three months later they took Jimmy to court. He told them his father was very ill, but he said that as far as they were concerned his father was getting better. They put Jimmy on probation. He still didn't attend school and eventually he had a home visit:

I did let them in, they saw my dad say for about five minutes and then they walked out, never to be heard from again.

It is through in-depth examination of the young carers' case histories that we discover the reality of the effects of caring on these children's lives. Nowhere are these effects more evident than in education where young carers continue to be neglected - even punished - for something which is beyond their control. The interviews illustrate that young carers are wary of coming to the attention of professionals or service providers. In terms of education, such wariness seems well founded. None of the school professionals adopted a flexible or sensitive approach to the young carers, nor did they offer them any support or look beyond the immediate problems at school once they had learned of their caring responsibilities .

Sarah was certainly a victim of this inflexible system. We discovered that Sarah could not read or write and she was eventually sent to a special school, but unfortunately this was some way from her home and was where she was the victim of an attack. Her father then refused to send her to school as he feared for her safety. The education authorities prosecuted him several times, but in the meantime Sarah became almost a recluse, spending all her time in the home caring for her mother. Sarah admitted that previously her caring duties meant she often took time off school and that when she did attend she was generally late:

> Because you've got to get ready, and I used to help my mum, get her up and then she wanted a pad putting on and stuff like that. I'd have to help her with that. So it was nearly all the time that I had to help my mum and that's why I was late.

Following the court battles, no further action was taken and yet Sarah missed two years of her education. At the time of interview, she was very concerned about her

lack of reading and writing ability, but she said the school authorities had 'just forgotten' about her.

Claire was fortunate in one sense in that she qualified for private tuition because she damaged her knee and had to take a year off school. This meant she could devote more attention to her mother, but it also meant her lifting tasks became more intense, which served to exacerbate the strain on her knee.

It is clear from the findings that what is lacking within education are staff and educational professionals who are going to pick up on noticeable stresses and strains on children who care; who can recognise and approach young carers on an individual basis, and offer their support.

The Best of Times, the Worst of Times
Clearly the effects of caring aren't confined simply to the physical or the practical. Caring can have long term repercussions on children's emotional development as well as on their aspirations. The stress produced by caring can induce depression, anxiety and fear, and yet all the young carers demonstrated a resilience that was quite remarkable.

It was quite clear from the interviews that young carers derived some positive feelings from caring; that there were certain facets to caring that served to reinforce their sense of self-worth, of being needed and loved. In this section we will explore these aspects and examine 'the best and worst of times' in caring.

During the interviews it became clear that a major effect of caring on children is limited horizons - young carers barely think further than the moment or tomorrow. Their dreams and plans for the future were confined within the caring environment.

Interestingly, none of the young carers talked a great deal about their future plans. When the subject of the future was introduced it was clear that the only plans the young carers had made concerned the welfare of the care receiver. Such a selfless perspective was undoubtedly influenced by the 'impossibility' of their lives; by the limits imposed on their lifestyles by the caring role; by the fact that caring confined them within the boundaries of the home, and presented them with few opportunities to view the future positively or with hope.

Notably, young carers' dreams for the future again related to their hopes and visions for their parent/s, as Claire said:

I have visions of my mum suddenly get up and walk down them stairs, but I know she won't ever. They've told her she'll never walk again.

The young carers' own work ambitions were restricted both by their caring responsibilities and their educational disadvantages (because they may not have performed well at school their opportunities were limited). Furthermore, their caring circumstances often seemed to confer on young carers a desire to continue in the caring role outside the home, not just because of the rewards associated with caring, but often because caring was all they had known. This was confirmed by the fact that five of the young carers wanted to go into nursing or a profession where they could 'help old or

young people'. For Claire, caring was the only worthwhile occupation:

If you can't look after somebody else, what can you do?

Four of the respondents were clearly uncertain about the direction of their lives because their caring roles had overwhelmed their dreams for the future and left them feeling confused. As Debra said: 'I was just screwy. I didn't know what I wanted to do - you don't have time to sort yourself out when you're caring for someone'.

Only Zia and Mansour knew exactly what they wanted to do when they left school, but their parents had encouraged them in their school work and had also tried to restrict the pressures imposed on them by their caring duties. However, Zia and Mansour's futures were to some extent determined by their commitment to care. For example, they had both decided that their plans to go to University would only be realised if they could go locally, and when the time came for them to leave home they had vowed to take their parents with them:

Even if we have to go away for a job then we'll take our parents with us. I think that when we were little mum and dad were ill and they could have sent us away, or put us with foster parents, but they didn't, they stood by us, so we'll do the same for them.
    (Zia)

Out of all the carers interviewed, only Jas

53

said he would leave his parents eventually, but only so he could earn some money and return later to take up his caring responsibilities once again.

Many of the young carers had already made a long-term commitment to care for their parent/s or, as in Gary's case, his brother. Gary had stated that he would care for his brother for the rest of his life, and he had ensured that his girlfriend also agreed to the lifelong care of his brother, or, he said, he wouldn't marry her!

Miriam had also committed herself to the full time care of her mother, until the time her mother died, or was hospitalised - only then would Miriam contemplate her own life, even though this meant a great deal of self-sacrifice and missed opportunity:

> *I think she might live another ten years, by which time I'll be 40. It'll be too late to have kids then. Maybe I'll travel the world, marry a millionaire and adopt loads of children!*
> (Miriam)

Once again we can account for the young carers' level of commitment to care in terms of socialisation and evaluation: they are socialised into their roles from a very early age and often have no other life experiences with which to evaluate their own caring existence. Although some of the young carers could remember a time when they weren't caring, for many of them it was difficult to recall what their lives had been like before the onset of the parental illness and their own caring responsibilities.

The focus of their memories on the whole, was once again confined within the boundaries of care. Diane started caring when she was about eight years old, but her memories before the onset of care were very vague:

> *I can't really remember - we've got photographs of holidays and things but I can't really remember.*

Jimmy remembered his life 'suddenly went down hill' with the onset of his father's illness, but he couldn't be specific about what his life had been like prior to the illness - his considerable responsibilities and the relentless caring routine had overshadowed his capacity to recall a time before care.

The level of commitment demonstrated by the young carers was even more striking considering their often painful and distressing experiences and considering the cycle of crises that affected their lives.

From the findings it emerged that the initial crisis point usually occurred with the onset of illness, especially if diagnosis was sudden and unexpected. However, often crises coincided, doubling the stress and anxiety suffered by the young carers. For example, Alison's father died suddenly when she was nine years old and shortly afterwards her mother was diagnosed with multiple sclerosis. Thus, Alison had to cope with grief (for her father) coupled with fear (for her mother's health):

> *I didn't want to know about mum's illness at first because I was so scared. It was horrible it really was. I thought I was going to lose my mum, I know it sounds stupid.*

Jimmy also had to cope with a double crisis - his parent's divorce and the diagnosis of his father's brain tumour. Indeed, for many of the young carers, the break up of their parent's marriage often seemed to coincide with the onset of illness and thus the onset of care. Such crises represent the 'worst of times' in the young carers' lives, and were often cyclical in nature. By this we mean that the caring process would run relatively smoothly for some time only to be interrupted by a crisis, usually relating to the care receiver's condition - a point of deterioration or an illness additional to the permanent one.

Interestingly, the 'worst of times' were described by the young carers only in relation to the care receiver's suffering and not their own problems or anxieties. However, clearly any factor which adversely affects the care receiver naturally increases the strain on young carers.

Again, one of the notable findings was the young carers' general acceptance of the bad times as 'storms to be weathered'. Only three of the carers interviewed had attempted to escape their situation by running away, and then only when conditions at home had become particularly difficult. For example, Debra ran away from her mother only when her mother's violence became too much for her to cope with. As we have already said, Jas ran away from home on several occasions because of the pressures of caring, but his absences from home served more as a respite from care and he always returned:

Dad will be really ill sometimes and sometimes I'll get pissed off about that. You just get so racked off...you just drop off to sleep and suddenly you hear him shouting for you. You never get two minutes on your own in this house, sometimes you think 'oh I've got to get some time by myself' and walk out...but I always come back.
(Jas)

Alison's own form of escape had been what she termed her 'rebellion' which was more emotional than physical as she tried to avoid the crisis at home. Even though she cared for her mother both physically and emotionally, initially she also resented her. During interview, Alison said she had overcome her rebellion and could see that it had been based on fear - the fear of losing her mother.

It was clear that the young carers would often sacrifice their personal feelings during the caring process and tried not to relay their own fears or depressions to the care receiver. They kept their personal mood swings private:

Some mornings I just don't want to get up. I assume it's just swings of moods, like sometimes I could cry all day and sometimes I'm happy all day, but I try and keep it to myself.
(Miriam)

It was also clear that in severe cases, despite the pain and distress caused by providing 24 hour care, young carers such as Linda and Jimmy, maintained their composure often until after care had finished. For example, Jimmy said that he 'cracked up' after his father died and Linda said she would have done the same if she hadn't been able to talk to someone about her loss. This was an important point - crises seemed to be more acute where the young carers were left alone to care. Sharing feelings, if not caring duties, with another person is a crucial factor in maintaining the welfare of young carers. Linda was fortunate in that she could share her grief with her brother:

> *On your own you would have cracked up under the pressure. It would have been too much. You wouldn't have been able to do it on your own.*
>   (Linda)

The problem is of course that help often comes too late or only during a crisis. For example Alison's family GP only asked her mother if she or Alison needed any bereavement counselling two years after Alisons's father had died, and, as we have already seen, social services only intervened in Debra's life when she ran away from home.

Jimmy was left alone to cope both during the caring period and afterwards. Indeed, his life was an endless circle of misery and crises. Following his father's death Jimmy lived alone in the house he had shared with his father, and went on weekly drinking binges, drove his father's car - even though he was not old enough to drive - and turned violent. Jimmy's grief, coupled with the fact that no one offered him any support, affected him severely:

> *Looking back on it I suppose I was a prat. I went to pieces. I was really getting drunk, it wasn't just moderate drinking.*

> *At first I went to pieces, I beat up a couple of my friends as soon as I got back from the hospital. I was so stupid I didn't know what to do. I smashed opposite neighbour's windows. But now things have changed quite a lot. You seem to try and forget everything, but you can't. Some nights I say to myself 'why did he have to die for?' and I get angry, but you can't carry on being anti-everyone.*

In terms of the effects of grief, we found no evidence to support Levin, Sinclair and Gorbach's (1983) suggestion that the greatest improvement in the mental health of the carer was the death or institutionalisation of the care receiver. Both Jimmy and Linda had suffered the loss of a parent for whom they were caring, and although the trauma of witnessing their deterioration had been removed, there was certainly no evidence that their psychological well being had been established following their parents' death.

Debra's mother had been institutionalised which had clearly distressed Debra, even though towards the end she wanted to be separated from her mother. However, whether because of the impact of her mother's condition and its potential risk for Debra, or because she had foregone her childhood to care for her mother, Debra's attitude and behaviour were both erratic and self-destructive following her mother's institutionalisation.

Clearly the young carers' status as children has an undoubted impact on the effects of loss and grief. For children, there will be the added impact of the loss of security, regardless of the arbitrary nature of this security due to their parents' dependency. Whatever the nature and extent of their caring responsibilities, the death of a parent for a child carer means they are deprived of a familiar psychological stronghold both in terms of the parental influence and the provision of care.

It was clear from the findings that in terms of crises young carers often suffered alone, without any outside support or comfort, but as we have already highlighted, it is often the case that only a small amount of support is needed to prevent further crises occurring.

In relation to the more emotive aspects of caring, from the young carer's perspective, it was clear that often it was not the above mentioned crises which affected the young carers most. Often their personal concerns focused on restrictions in the caring relationship, such as activities the young carers could not enjoy with their parents because of the nature of the particular illness or disability. For example, Zia and Mansour wanted to be able to play cricket with their father, but his arthritis prevented it. Alison wanted to go out for walks with her mother 'like other children go out with their parents' but she knew she couldn't.

It was clear from the findings however that there were positive aspects of caring. In some cases it seemed the caring responsibility conferred on some young carers a sense of self-worth; of being needed and loved. Often though these young carers had known little other than the caring experience and it was the one area in their lives that they could locate a sense of self-worth or satisfaction. As Sarah explained:

I like helping mum. It's really good to be with her all the time. To talk to her. She likes someone to talk to.

However, we know that Sarah had cared for some considerable time and that her activities were confined to the home and the caring environment. She didn't have any friends, she didn't go to school and she could neither read or write. In effect, caring for her mother was all she had.

Gary actually said he loved caring for his brother for the emotional rewards it afforded him (although it must be stressed that Gary was not solely responsible for the care of his brother in that his parents also offered their support):

I enjoy it all. I get so much attention from him and affection. It's like going through life on a ultimate high. I don't think you could get affection like that from any other child. It's not possible. Like able-bodied children, they're just not the same, they get into trouble, they fight, but with my brother there's none of that it's just pure love and attention. It's fantastic.
    (Gary)

Considering that the greatest need expressed by the young carers was for someone to talk to (see chapter six), it is perhaps not surprising that the young carers derived some sense of self-worth from the caring experience. Often the care receiver was all the young carers had. Giving constant attention to their welfare instilled in them a sense of being needed, as Diane said:

I like the fact I'm helping my mum. It makes me feel that I'm doing something for somebody and not just moping around the place.

The Caring Relationship

Even though in young caring, the roles have been reversed in that the child becomes the parent of the parent, it is still the parent-child experience that is important. Even though the child has undertaken caring responsibility for the parent, their existence in the home as parental figures is crucial.

None of the young or adult carers talked about the care receiver in terms of dependency (which is partly why we have chosen not to use the term 'dependant' in this report). Pragmatically the roles might have been reversed, but emotionally their parents' status as guardians remained intact. This could explain why the young carers demonstrated such a high level of commitment to their parents and why the loss of a parent was not of immediate psychological benefit to the young carer as was discussed earlier. Thus we can see that the young carers' burden of responsibility was only a practical responsibility, and not a burden in terms of their emotional and psychological relationship with their parents.

From the findings it was not easy to distinguish distinct patterns in the caring relationship between care provider and care receiver, as individual cases varied so much. However, a gender-related pattern emerged between female providers and recipients of care. When both were female, the caring experience seemed to consolidate a bond of affection and commitment, although this might have been because the girls interviewed found it easier to talk about their emotional relationships.

It was also possible to identify an initial period of adjustment in the caring relationship, sometimes reflected in a period of scepticism and mistrust. For example, when Miriam and Debra started caring for their mothers, initially they refused to believe in the illness and thought their mothers were 'putting it on'. This reluctance to accept the truth of their disabilities perhaps had its roots in fear. Even though the reality of their mothers' illnesses were obvious, Miriam and Debra still chose to believe they were lying about their conditions. Debra even tried to set traps for her mother:

Like when we used to live over in Primrose Avenue she said she could not walk, but I thought she could. I used to put her fags on the top shelf and when I got home from school she'd be smoking and I'd think well how did she get them?

Or Miriam:

When I was young and at school and mum was in a wheelchair I used to think that she just hated housework and when we were out the house she was walking about and everything. And I used to think if I come home early one day I'll catch her - one of my other sisters thought that as well I found out later.

Another effect of caring in terms of the caring relationship was an initial period of resentment or even hatred by the young carers towards the care receiver, although this was rarely communicated to the care receiver themselves. It was something the young carers successfully concealed. Again, one could account for this resentment in fear - fear of the future, fear of the unknown, fear of being different, even fear of the loss of the parent as well as resentment that their lives would be adversely affected by the caring role:

> *I know it sounds horrible, but I hated my mum at first because I felt like it was her fault that I had to do these things, which now I know it's not her fault. And I was frightened I was going to lose her.*
> (Alison)

Where the caring responsibility on the young carer was intense, this would inevitably intensify emotional relations between the young carer and the care receiver. Although one-to-one caring often resulted in particular stresses, it also seemed to heighten commitment between care recipient and provider, and this did not depend on a good relationship prior to the onset of caring.

As we have already indicated, this closeness, or synergy seemed to be more prevalent between the girls and their mothers, although Jimmy was most candid about his close relationship with his father. It seemed that isolation also invoked commitment and bonding. Jimmy, Alison and Diane all had very good relationships with their parents, and all managed their caring responsibilities on their own.

Debra's relationship with her mother on the other hand was never good, in fact it deteriorated during the caring process. However, here the nature of the care receiver's condition was a determining factor in the caring relationship because Debra's mother's condition adversely affected her behaviour. Debra's hatred for her mother was inspired by her mother's violent outbursts and it was only when the two were separated that the relationship improved, because the threat of violence had been removed:

> *I used to hate her, really hate her. One time when we had an argument...I hit her with a brush because I hated her so much. She was beating me so I just turned round and got this brush...I just smacked her with it. The only thing that's brought us closer together was when she went into the home, because when she went there she realised I was her daughter and what she had done to me and she's sorry now. But it's too late.*
> (Debra)

What was most revealing was the young carers' capacity for understanding and forbearing both in terms of the caring process and their relationship with the care receiver. Such forbearance was evident in the young carers' capacity for understanding, even when caring was made difficult. For example, Debra said that she understood her mother's illness was the cause of her violent behaviour, even though she hated her at the time. Miriam was equally understanding about her mother even though she often seemed to be an ungrateful recipient of her care:

She moans a lot. She thinks I'm bad
tempered all the time. She treats me like a
child sometimes. I want to feel that she
loves me sometimes, but I don't. I do
think this is because of her illness. She
gets bad tempered because I can do
things she can't.
   (Miriam)

Conclusion

It is clear that the effects of caring on children can often be very painful and distressing. Their social, emotional and educational opportunities are undermined by the constant demands made on them through caring. They often have to forego their childhood as well as their personal and work-related ambitions, and their lives are restricted by the geographical and psychological boundaries of the caring environment.

Despite all these factors, young carers continue to demonstrate a remarkable commitment and affection for their sick or disabled loved ones, and indeed often under the most extreme and arduous circumstances, manage to derive some positive feedback from their caring roles. They do so in spite of the crises they go through and in spite of the lack of outside comfort and provision.

Expressed Needs of Young Carers 6

Introduction

In this chapter we will examine the expressed needs of young carers in terms of formal services, information needs and emotional support. However, it is important to emphasise that the young carers did not talk about their needs specifically in terms of the above defined categories. They did not for example highlight gaps in service provision, but rather talked more emotively about what their immediate psychological needs were.

As Alderson (1992:169) points out, children can often be less able in pointing out gaps and contradictions in services, because of their lack of understanding about policy and also because they are excluded from discussions about service planning. As young carers issues are not included in recent community care policy guidelines, and as present policy on client-based services (such as CCA's and community nursing - see chapter four) is also unclear and inconsistent, it is perhaps not surprising that the young carers are also confused.

What was evident was that these children are in urgent need of support - particularly advice and information - and above all emotional and psychological comfort and reassurance. Currently no one is listening to young carers; but no one is talking to them either.

Formal Professional Support

Many of the young and adult carers' families were already receiving some form of client-based support for the care receiver (see chapter four) and most of them had realistic expectations about its limitations. Young carers were aware that help could not be provided 24-hours a day, or perhaps when they needed it most - throughout the night. More importantly, many of them had reached a stage where they had been so long without adequate support that they no longer wanted what they would term 'interference' in their lives.

Most of the young carers had cared for some considerable time in isolation and had adjusted to the idea of managing alone. Arguably, if services are going to intervene to provide for the child and promote their civil rights, then they should do so before this period of adjustment gets underway.

Specific expressed needs in terms of practical help was very much dependent on individual cases and the nature of the care receiver's condition. Thus, from the young carers perspectives practical needs tended to focus on the needs of the care receiver, although clearly any support that improved the quality of life for the care receiver would, to some extent, have a beneficial effect on the lives of the carers. For example, Claire's immediate practical requirement was to obtain a bungalow for the family so her mother could get to the toilet and the bedroom on her own. The immediate benefit to Claire would be that she would not have to lift her mother, and consequently prevent further strain on her knee.

Jas and Alison wanted more help in the home 'generally', and some such as Zia and Mansour needed help of a more specific nature, for example for major household jobs such as the decorating and 'big jobs that we can't do yet'.

Out of all the carers interviewed only Manoj and Jimmy mentioned financial support. Although Jimmy's father was in receipt of various disability allowances, these took some time to be processed which meant Jimmy had to 'beg' for food parcels in the meantime:

> *When Dad first got diagnosed with his brain tumour, it took months for the attendance allowance to come, that's something that should be helped - speed the money up, it took about five and a half months for the money to come through, which it isn't very good, by then it's too late and anything could have happened.*
> (Jimmy)

Manoj simply stated that he needed money generally, rather than outside help. Young caring, like most informal care, is essentially unpaid work and often young carers forgo incomes that many other children are able to receive through part-time paid employment. Thus young carers are effectively disenfranchised from the labour market. Manoj simply did not have the time, nor perhaps the inclination to take on any extra work, because of the extent of his caring responsibilities.

As we have already indicated the young carers did not express their needs in terms of formal support, or highlighting gaps in present services. They did not discuss the potential for flexible approaches or the sensitive representation of children's rights. However, such concepts and ideas formed the basis of some of their thoughts. For example Debra talked about an ideal situation which would have benefited both herself and her mother, and which was based on a flexible

approach to service provision:

> *I think if it is a one parent family like my mum was, like we were, then there should be some way for that person's child to be able to go in the home with the person. I think that's a good idea. So they can care for them when they want, but also be looked after as well.*

Not one of the carers interviewed expressed their formal needs in terms of a social worker or named professionals from specific agencies. This may have been because of the general distrust demonstrated towards social workers, based on experience or expectation. It may also have been because of the fear of the consequences of inviting such professionals into their lives. It was also evident that both young and adult carers alike didn't trust social workers or other such professionals to be discrete or trustworthy. As Miriam said:

> *I wouldn't want a social worker. It's too official. Also you think it's going to get back to your mother.*

It is clear that any form of professional intervention aimed at supporting young carers would have to be a) independent from any recognised authority or agency, b) entirely confidential, c) sensitively managed, d) based on the expressed needs of young carers, and any discussion with their families sanctioned by the young carers themselves. It was also clear during the interviews that any professional involvement in the young carers lives would have to be based on an understanding of the young caring experience. As Debra said:

> Not a social worker who's going to patronise you and who don't know what they are talking about apart from what they have read in books.

Information Needs

'Information is now widely recognised as the key to helping dependent older people and their carers to improve the quality of their lives in the community' (Tester, 1992:1).

It was clear that information was an essential need among both the young and adult carers. Interestingly, the carers did not want information concerning their own needs, but advice and support on care management and medical information relating to the care receiver's condition. None of the young carers seemed to have any understanding of the potential sources of information, bearing out Tester's (1992:1) argument that carers are often unaware of community care services available or where to get hold of information. All the young carers said they wanted 'someone' to advise them, to inform them about the care receiver's diagnosis and prognosis and to reassure them that their caring skills were both effective and satisfactory.

It is essential to ascertain what information sources young carers were utilising. In terms of the practical aspects of caring, as we have already seen in chapter three, no one instructed or provided the young carers with information on lifting techniques or on other practical aspects of caring.

Equally, none of the young carers had been given any information about benefits or access to services, either for themselves (because there are no services specifically targeted at young carers) or the care receivers. In short, the dissemination of information by professionals among young carers was non existent. Clearly, in order to provide for young carers effectively, they must first be recognised as carers with distinct needs, and as we have already seen, young carers are effectively ignored.

If we consider Doyle and Harding's argument (1992:75), that an agency's commitment to treating carers with dignity and respect is reflected in the quality of information available to them, then young carers are effectively denied professional respect, because information provision is non existent.

The interviews revealed that information needs were generally expressed by the young and adult carers alike in terms of medical information. The dissemination and accessibility of medical information is it seems crucial to carer well being. However, in terms of medical knowledge both young and adult carers currently live their lives in a state of unwitting naiveté.

There has been a great deal of work on the delivery of medical information to children, especially where the illness/condition of a parent has a high risk factor in relation to the child/ren - conditions such as Huntington's Chorea (HC) or HIV/AIDS. As we have already highlighted, the nature of such conditions imposes the adoption of a child's perspective.

Considering the nature of such conditions

63

as HC or HIV/AIDS, children must be involved in communication processes with trained professionals who can administer support and disseminate information with consideration and sensitivity. It seems that the same focus does not apply to young carers, and yet information both diagnostically and prognostically is crucial, as it has a direct impact on their lives as carers. However, as Honigsbaum (1991:82) points out: 'Direct communication with the clients is a neglected area of work in all aspects of services for children'.

Work in the US and indeed elsewhere on HIV and AIDS has focused on the need for professionals to promote the rights of children and to ensure their needs are met. Such work has stated that health information should be age appropriate, brief, clear and differentiated; it should elicit feedback from children, give hope and integrate information into the child's setting, inducing willingness to hear. Also, educators should joke, using humour judiciously to 'diffuse anxiety and discomfort' (Honigsbaum, 1991:55).

Considering the nature and extent of care provided by the young and adult carers, their lack of understanding in relation to the care receiver's condition was striking. This was true across the board. Indeed, multiple sclerosis - one of the most common disabilities - affected four out of the 15 families and in each case the carers had very little understanding of the condition. For example, Miriam only found out from a friend at school what the initials 'MS' meant, but even then she did not fully understand the implications of her mother's condition, and her mother would not discuss it with her:

I can't remember who told me it was multiple sclerosis, and I still didn't know what it was - well you don't do you?
 (Miriam)

One would certainly not expect a child to understand the medical complexities of multiple sclerosis without adequate instruction. However, when it affects their lives so manifestly, young carers have a right to comprehensive medical information so that they can organise their caring responsibilities and their personal futures, as well as further their own psychological preparation for long term care.

Furthermore, it is not reasonable to expect that such information should come from the care receiver. It was clear from the findings that often both the care receiver and the young carer did not want to discuss the particular medical condition because of the pain and distress involved. In certain cases, such reluctance was also a result of misunderstanding on both parts ie that neither the young carer nor the care receiver fully understood the nature of the specific condition.

The provision of information must also take account of a young carer's reluctance to access medical information. Although information was a commonly expressed need among both young and adult carers, it was clear that some of the youngsters were afraid of the consequences of learning too much about their parent's condition.

Both Alison and Diane revealed a distinct reluctance to learn more about multiple sclerosis. Alison's mother had told her to go to the family doctor for her information -

Alison said she did go but that she didn't listen. Diane was also very unsure about finding out too much:

> I don't know, I don't think I would want to know how it's going to progress, how much worse it's going to get because we might be looking into the future and thinking how bad it's going to get and not thinking how it is at the moment.
> (Diane)

However, Diane said 'general' information about multiple sclerosis would have benefited her. It might also, if delivered appropriately and sensitively, have allayed some of her worst fears.

Information has to be delivered by trained individuals who have the time and expertise to talk to young carers properly, who will understand their needs and be able to allay their fears. Chapter four revealed that GP's are not ideally placed to deliver information to young carers due to constraints on their time and the nature of practice (in the consulting room under pressure). Furthermore, it is clear that GP's are not identifying young carers or their needs in their work.

Claire was in a particularly difficult situation because her mother's condition remained undiagnosed. Doctors could not in effect relieve Claire's worries as they too were uncertain of the nature of her mother's condition. However, because of this Claire had been forced to surmise or guess the nature of her mother's condition. No one had explained to her - even after years of tests on her mother - which conditions had been ruled out:

> At first I thought it was MS, but now I don't think so because that gets you straight away, but this is so gradual. Now I think it's muscular dystrophy. I've read about it and it's passed on through the genes, but there's no history of it in our family.
> (Claire)

Sarah also continued to care for her mother in the same degree of confusion. Although the family doctor initially visited the family to explain about multiple sclerosis, he spoke to her father and not to Sarah. Thus Sarah's medical information came via her father:

> He just said the doctor had said it's pretty bad and if we could help her through the years. But she's not doing anything, not moving, I don't know.
> (Sarah)

Although levels of understanding undoubtedly increased as the carers got older, it did not necessarily follow that the adult carers were satisfied with the information they had received. It was clear that although adult carers had access to more professional help in relation to the care receiver and they felt more confident about asking for support (for example, Sally only requested community care assistance for her mother when Sally was in her 20s with a family to support) in terms of medical information they were as unaware as the young carers.

For example, Linda received a great deal

of nursing support for her mother who had breast cancer, but she still received no medical advice or information, nor was she provided with any details about her mother's prognosis:

> *I needed some advice or guidelines from someone on what to expect. You just did not know what to expect. Maybe they don't know the signs, I don't know. I think they could prepare you a bit more, let you know what's going on a bit more, talk to you. We never had doctors come to us and tell us what was going on or what they had done.*
> (Linda)

Gary suffered similar confusion and anxiety. His brother was not in receipt of medical treatment as he had been brain damaged since birth, but he developed certain behavioural problems in later life which were the cause of some concern to Gary. However, he did not know who to turn to for advice: 'social services or a child psychologist, I just don't know where to turn'. He said he wanted 'a professional' to help, but could find none and his doctor was too busy:

> *I think they could be a bit more helpful, even if it was just a written pamphlet saying who you could get in touch with for these sort of things. It would be a bigger improvement on having nothing at all.*
> (Gary)

Jimmy's was perhaps the saddest case of all. He wanted to care for his father and did so against many odds (socio economic deprivation, lack of support, prosecution), but no one had provided him with a medical prognosis in relation to his father's condition. Although the doctors and specialists may not have been able to predict exactly what the effects of his father's brain tumour might have been, they could have indicated the *possible* effects - medical staff could have engaged Jimmy in discussions about the possible outcomes of his father's condition. However, as Jimmy said: 'The fits, I wasn't told anything of the sort. That was the worst thing. No one said fits'. (Jimmy's father's first fit occurred while he was driving the family car - Jimmy was in the passenger seat at the time).

It is clear that information is a crucial commodity for young and adult carers alike, and it is hard to imagine the reasons for the persistent neglect of their information needs. At the very least carers have a right to choose whether to access information networks, and they must be provided with adequate diagnostic and prognostic information in relation to the care receiver's condition. They must also have access to information about benefits and services available to themselves as carers and their loved ones as the recipients of care.

Someone to Talk To

'Information should [also] inform them of how to obtain independent advice and information and should include a named individual to whom they can go for counselling or advice' (Honigsbaum, 1991:82).

Nowhere is the need for this more

applicable than for young carers, whose basic human need is clearly being denied them - a need described simply as 'someone to talk to'. Young carers were often isolated as carers and those people who might possibly provide 'a shoulder to cry on' (for example family and close friends) were often remarkably unsupportive in terms of their emotional needs (see chapter four).

We have already examined the effects of caring on social life and friendships in chapter five, and seen that young carers are often reluctant to talk about their problems or their circumstances to others. However, they would clearly be willing to talk if encouraged to do so in a sensitive and understanding manner. Indeed, every one of the young and adult carers specifically stated that what they needed most was 'someone to talk to', either when times were bad, for advice on aspects of care management, or more usually as a friend, confidante or advocate.

All the young and adult carers identified 'someone to talk to' as a specific and essential need and even those in a family situation where other adults could also provide care, such as Gary (whose parents were also able to care for his brother), still needed outside support for friendship or advice:

When I came home after a year away I just didn't know which way to turn with my brother because he'd got that far out of hand. Sometimes now it would be nice to talk to someone to see what they could do, or how they could advise me.
    (Gary)

It was also clear that a confidante, or advocate had to be both independent (ie not connected to recognised agencies, nor to family networks and friends) and trustworthy. These were seen to be essential criteria, for as we have seen, both family and friends as well as professionals were often unreliable and not always to be trusted. For example, both Sarah and Claire had friends in the past who they had anticipated might be potential 'confidantes', but who abandoned them at a later date (ie when their caring duties affected their ability to socialise). We have also seen that often friends did not understand the nature of the caring experience. This is perhaps why *all* the young carers who said they needed 'someone to talk to' also said they must be someone 'who had been through the same experience' - preferably someone who had been a young carer themselves or who understood exactly what was involved in caring.

Ideally it would be someone who'd cared themselves because they know what you're going through. Because they've already cared they could help you talk things out.
    (Diane)

Or Linda:

Just someone to talk to who had been through the same thing.

Miriam:

Maybe I could have told somebody that I was going into my room and crying because I thought my mum was trying to drive me mad and maybe someone else felt the same thing and could tell me what they did about it.

As we have already indicated the independence and trustworthiness of the advocate would be essential. This was clear from the fact that some carers worried about issues of confidentiality and some wanted to obtain help 'anonymously' to ensure their privacy:

With a helpline you can be anonymous if you want to. You can just ask for help in certain areas. You don't have to say who you are or who your parent is. You don't have to give a name and address, just ask for help and advice from somebody.
(Miriam)

Miriam also recognised that such support, if provided early in caring could prevent or relieve future problems:

If there was somebody you could ask advice from maybe things wouldn't be so bad when you were older.

Although previous research and especially the work of the Carers National Association Young Carers Project has focused on providing a contact point for young carers, and organising young carers networks, it was clear from our findings that such strategies should be self-determined, and that in reality young carers preferred a one-to-one encounter with a trained, or understanding individual. As Jimmy said: 'If there was a one-to-one basis then that's fine, but if it's a big group then no'.

It appeared that some of the young carers wanted an advocate or confidante to befriend them on a long-term basis. As Alison explained:

It would be like a best mate helping me wouldn't it? Once you'd got to know the person sort of thing - they'd know what you were on about and could be your friend for a long time.

This need for empathy from an independent individual was clearly very important to the young carers as was the need for someone to understand their innermost feelings. As Debra said:

If someone was talking to me and had been through it they wouldn't just know what I'm saying but they'd know how I'm feeling inside, do you understand?

A system or scheme not dissimilar from the 'Buddying' scheme for people with HIV/ AIDS seems to be one of the most appropriate advocacy models which could provide for the needs of young carers. The 'buddying' concept was developed in America as a response to the clearly expressed needs of people with HIV/AIDS, and it seems that this model could be readily applied to respond to the needs of young carers as clients. As well as befriending, 'buddying' also offers practical help and support and the 'buddies' themselves are trained to deal competently and sensitively with the complex nature of the condition and its effects.

Conclusion

Regardless of the liberation or protection argument, we must provide adequately for young carers' needs and this provision must be made on the basis of their expressed requirements. Arguably, young carers are an inevitable reality of so-called informal community care, whether such care is provided openly or covertly. 'Buddying' would relieve the stress and anxiety of caring by providing young carers with support in relation to their most urgent needs and prevent them from remaining hidden and neglected in the community.

With appropriate training in issues relating specifically to children who care - including welfare rights advice, the provision of information (medical information and advice on benefits and care management), as well as advocacy and representation - the 'Buddy' could become a lifeline for young carers (the scheme already runs successfully in Nottingham for people with HIV/AIDS) and might prevent the isolation and distress of young carers such as Jimmy:

> *The problem was not having anyone to talk to. If someone had come round and asked how I was that would have made a change. But there was nothing like that.*

7 Interviews with Professionals

Introduction

Recent research has found that awareness of young carers was limited among professionals and service providers (see Bilsborrow, 1992). From our research it would seem that the same is still true today. The interviews conducted for this research with professionals from health, education, social services and voluntary sector organisations and groups were initially intended to identify young carers and also to ascertain the level of awareness of the young caring issue. They were also designed to assess the professionals' knowledge of present services, or potential innovations which could incorporate welfare provision for children who care.

Twigg noted the differences in how professionals conceptualise carers services (1989) and found that not only were there inter departmental distinctions, but also differences within the hierarchy of professionals (ie that front line practitioners for example will have different views on carers issues from those in higher management due to the dynamics of various hierarchical pressures). Such distinctions were confirmed during the interviews with professionals. For example, one manager from social services when asked about attitudes to children who care, said:

As a department we have a duty to promote the child's welfare throughout their childhood, but there is a difference of course between different departments, between say the child care domain and other departments, as well as differences in attitude.

However, in terms of levels of awareness of the reality of young caring, it emerged that across the board - irrespective of division or professional status - awareness was limited. However, it also appeared that awareness was to some extent determined by the level of personal interest or experience. For example, some of those interviewed were aware of young caring as an issue because they could identify themselves in the caring role:

I've always been aware of it, maybe through the press, but I suppose I identified myself as being a young carer.
(Carers services development worker)

The interviews clearly revealed the covert nature of young carers, both as a group of informal workers and as a target for service provision. However once the issue was introduced, certain ideas and proposals did emerge about the effects of caring on children and the implications for service providers.

Awareness and Identification

It must be stressed that over half of those professionals interviewed were connected in some way through the project's steering group, so awareness in such cases was pre-determined. Among those professionals outside the steering group who had no personal knowledge of young carers, the degree of misunderstanding and false assumption was considerable as was their inability to regard young carers as a distinct group with specific needs. As one social services child care professional commented:

It would be interesting to know [about young carers] but I don't really see that there's a need for a new range of services, everything's going to be reduced in the present economic climate. I think it's more to do with presentation, to say: 'look we're not out to take your kid away'.

Within social services, especially in the child care domain, there was a lack of awareness of young carers as 'an encapsulated group' and understanding on a managerial level was circumscribed by generic notions of carers, for example:

You shouldn't get into categorising, you should look at the totality, pressure groups occasionally bring them to our attention, sometimes rightly so. There's a number of people jumping around about the issue of young carers.

As we have already acknowledged, awareness among professionals was to a large extent determined by personal knowledge or experiential factors. Certainly the most strident among the professionals interviewed was a disabled worker whose daughter had started caring for her at a very young age:

Something has got to be done about children who care. My daughter was caring for me when she was a very young child and I did everything I could to get outside support, but as long as it's known there's someone in the house who can provide help, then outside support is not as forthcoming.

Those professionals involved in developing carers services were clearly aware of the issue but identification of specific young carers for research purposes remained problematic (as one worker suggested, it was difficult enough identifying adult carers). Even after enquiries had been made among colleagues - social workers in the field - about the potential for identification, the issue still remained a difficult one. As one development worker pointed out: 'Some social workers who go into families where a child is caring just don't see it'.

A revealing inter-departmental tension was noted in education between lower and higher management professionals. On a lower management level those interviewed were aware of young carers through their work, although as one education welfare officer pointed out, when she did encounter young carers in school, she often felt powerless to help them effectively. However, we were unable to contact young carers through education channels because of difficulties with co-operation. The research process would have benefited from the co-operation of the education authority and access to young carers through educational channels. It is hoped that we will be able to pursue and document the experiences of young carers with educational difficulties in a later project.

Those professionals who had direct personal experience of young caring or who had met young carers in their work were far more vociferous in their approach to the issue and often demonstrated anger and frustration over the lack of support or recognition for young carers:

I've been trying to do something about young carers for twenty years. The attitude is that as long as there's somebody in the house you're seen as easy pickings. My home help was cut down because my daughter was 14 and could take on the extra role.

(voluntary sector advisor for people with disabilities)

(Interestingly this same point emerged several times during interviews with young carers, but service providers denied community care assistance would be withdrawn once a child reached what seemed to be an arbitrarily determined 'responsible' age - see section on community care assistance in chapter four).

Consequences of Caring - Considering the Issues

Once the issue of young carers had been introduced among professionals, a discussion ensued about the consequences of young caring. Again, clear departmental distinctions emerged, especially in social services between those connected with or responsible for services to children and services to elderly people. The disparity here focused on the fundamental rights of the child on the one hand and the concerns of imposing familial norms on the other.

This latter point was at the forefront of discussion in child care services and related specifically to the issue of young carers performing intimate tasks for an adult care receiver. Concern was expressed that highlighting the levels of intimate caring responsibilities among young carers would

invoke 'moral outrage', as one child care professional commented:

If you say there are 50 kids in Nottinghamshire who wipe their parents bums...there is a risk of outsiders imposing their own family norms on these families. I don't think it's a problem if the kid and parent are at ease with that.

Although it was clear from the findings that some young carers had been undertaking such intimate caring responsibilities for many years - and will continue to do so through lack of adequate support - and although these young carers may have adapted to their roles as 'private nurses', a humanitarian perspective would ask if it is right that they should *have* to adapt to this role? As one carers development worker suggested, levels of embarrassment must be examined as well as the conditions of care:

The age the child started caring may also have considerable impact. If as a young carer you've been performing intimate caring tasks since you can remember you may have adjusted to it in your own environment, but what about outside the family, when something tells you you're different?

Although it may be true, as the aforementioned child care practitioner suggested 'There are kids in much worse situations than changing the parent's nappy if you like', there has to be some consideration for human pride and dignity. Even if the young carer has adapted - perhaps unwillingly - to the idea of assisting with her/his parent's toileting, for example, the care receiver's feelings about their child performing such intimate tasks for them must also be understood. In our research we did not find one young carer who said they or their parent found the performance of intimate tasks, such as toileting, acceptable.

The response from social services professional workers with elderly people relating to children's intimate caring responsibilities was at variance with the perspective of those responsible for children's provision. One practitioner noted:

We should not expect a child to do anything a child in a 'normal' family household would not do, yes they should assist in modest ways, keep their room tidy, light tasks...but we should not expect the child to take the main responsibility for running the show.

This perspective was mirrored by those professionals who had personal experience of young caring or who had encountered young carers in their work. It was clear that the division between, for example child care services and other sector workers was embodied in a human rights argument. The prevailing conviction adhered to by those professionals outside the child care domain was the 'rights of the child' principle and reflected the spirit of the 1989 Children Act, which suggests that in decision making the child's wishes and feelings should be determined. As one disabled coalition officer commented:

Do we know what the child thinks about

carrying out intimate tasks? Why should a kid of 14 change his mother's sanitary towel? We're supposed to be a nation of child lovers and yet we abuse them, we criticise the Romanians but we simply have to look in our own backyards.

What *is* surprising, however, is that it was professionals working outside the child care arena who were prioritising the 'children's rights' argument. It was this debate surrounding children's rights and what was acceptable or inadmissible in terms of informal caring by children which instigated a closer examination in the research of the execution of intimate caring tasks by young carers (see chapter three).

Choice, Chance and Communication

A common theme which emerged during the interviews with the professionals was the notion of *choice* and its relevance to children in undertaking the caring role. Those who had encountered young carers in their work or who had personal experience of young caring were adamant that young carers had no choice in commencing the caring role, that indeed these children are 'lumbered with caring'. (See also box 1).

Another prominent theme which emerged was that young carers often come to the attention of professionals by *chance*. This was reasoned in terms of young carers' own determined silence - their 'reluctance to tell' - as one professional suggested: 'children tend not to share bad experiences'. Or it was also proposed that these children might find it difficult to talk to adults and teachers, through fear and their inability to recognise themselves as carers.

It was also suggested that once a young carer had come to the attention of professionals, a further obstacle to welfare provision was the lack of *communication* between agencies. Yet as Meredith (1992) points out, innovation and communication between agencies are vital. Education practitioners echoed this sentiment suggesting it was imperative that those professionals involved with families should communicate any problems to the education authorities (although this presupposes that such professionals recognise and communicate with the child/ren at the point of contact with the family). One education welfare officer explained:

> We tend to stumble across the young carers and it's not the right way. It should be diagnosed within the family, and then there has to be some communication of the problems involved with the school.

The health professionals also highlighted this need for inter-professional co-operation. As one medical officer remarked during interview, families were fortunate indeed if they had access to a good GP who would observe the child's caring role because 'they usually don't take children as carers in their sphere of interest'. There was also a suggestion that adult and children's services should be linked in some way because presently, the woman who has multiple sclerosis for example is the patient and yet the child who is carrying her up the stairs regularly, 'does not come into it'.

Some Solutions

When considering notions of welfare provision for young carers, many professionals talked in terms of assessment and how to reconcile limited funding with unrestricted access. There were many references to the lack of resources and the reductions in present services, indeed to many of the professionals interviewed, the idea of creating new services seemed inappropriate in light of the 'present economic climate'.

Legislation would seem to support this view. For example, the guidance accompanying the NHS and Community Care Act 1990 confers on local authorities the power to make their own judgements when assessing needs but suggests services should be provided 'within available resources'. However, as Doyle and Harding point out (1992) this notion is being challenged and some local authorities are accepting that services must be provided irrespective of the ability to finance them.

Much discussion centred on assessment and the difficulties of determining a young carer's needs. But as one professional involved in developing services for carers pointed out:

> You have to assess young carers, if not you're not going to meet their needs. Workers must pick up on stresses and strains within the family and make referrals where necessary.

Reflecting on the rights of children, some of the professionals interviewed argued that on a basic level it is necessary to allow children who care the opportunity to express their views, as well as provide them with any relevant information they may require. It was considered imperative that these young carers, at the very least, have access to 'someone they can talk to'. As one education welfare officer said of her experience with a young carer in school: 'When she realised I was going to listen then she came to me regularly.'

Generally, the professional perspective in terms of provision for young carers was that it was easier to talk hypothetically than to provide examples of existing services, which could adequately incorporate provision for children who care. One co-ordinator for disabled services commented:

> There is nothing to address the needs of the child. It is assumed they will take on the role of child care, and there is nothing to support them in that role. The money is there and it is imperative we make sure there is sufficient care to remove the responsibilities from the children.

It was impossible to determine any coherent policy recommendations for assessing and providing for young carers simply from interviews with the professionals. For many, these interviews represented the first time they had considered or discussed young carers. Attitudes towards provision seemed to be based either on human rights issues or were informed by fiscal considerations. However, within social services, elderly sector professionals could identify baseline principles for intervention, even though definitions had yet to be developed:

> If a parent can't perform a task that a child should not be doing, then statutory or support services should then begin to have a role. We have to grope for some sort of norm of family life and apply that with some sensitivity...we have got to think of the child's welfare, there are things they can't do or shouldn't do even if they are bursting to do them.

Conclusion

The contemporaneous nature of young caring as an issue and as a reality was reflected in the interviews with the service professionals. Levels of awareness were limited among those who had not encountered young caring in their work. Those who had contact with young carers asserted that these children were isolated, neglected and had little choice in undertaking the caring role.

In terms of service provision there seemed to be a yawning chasm between what services are currently available and what should be available - resources allowing. Within certain sectors, among those professionals who had not encountered young carers in their work, levels of understanding were limited, and yet many false assumptions were made about present methods of identifying and supporting children who care . As one professional from social services working in child care reported: 'If the adult is disabled, professionals will always take into account the pressures on the rest of the family.' The evidence reported here suggests that this is not the case when the pressures on the rest of the family are borne by young carers.

8 Conclusions and Actions

In all parts of the world many children suffer a serious shortfall in the basic prerequisites for autonomous and healthy development, yet social indicators of this lack are woefully inadequate.
(Doyal and Gough, 1991:206)

Nowhere is the above point perhaps more true than in relation to young carers. The findings reported here reveal that there are no societal markers which highlight the circumstances and needs of children who care. These children are effectively overlooked by professionals and often neglected by family and friends, and yet these young carers reveal a remarkable commitment to the care (and indeed the continuation of care) of their loved ones, often at the expense of their own ambitions and aspirations - indeed often at the expense of their own childhood.

The foundations are laid in legislation for children to be listened to and for their rights to be observed. But the needs of young carers continue to be neglected. Their very status as children reinforces their powerlessness and their status as carers is denigrated - their experiences and needs often shrouded in a veil of mystery and silence.

We have seen that children who care are denied the rights and opportunities that other children enjoy - the right to play, social interaction and friendships, education, autonomy - the opportunities to be children.

A World Health Organisation study (1982) identified four categories of need in relation to children's development: the need for love and security; the need for new experience; praise and recognition; and the need to be able to gradually extend their responsibilities in the family environment. Our findings reveal that most, if not all of these needs were often undermined by the caring experience.

As carers, many children can feel loved and needed. Indeed, their ability to derive positive feedback from many aspects of caring was quite striking. Even from the most painful and difficult circumstances, they were able to express feelings of self-worth and love. However, 'love' in this sense was often only forthcoming from the caring relationship - from the care receivers themselves. For as we have seen, the potential for protection, consideration or appreciation from other family members and friends was extremely limited.

Young caring certainly does not appear to promote feelings of security. Young carers are beset with anxieties and fears: fear for their parent/s health or well being; fear of coming to the attention of paid professionals; the loss associated with the death or institutionalisation of the loved one; the uncertainty of their futures - all these aspects serve to generate and nurture feelings of insecurity.

It was also evident that young carer's access to new experience was severely impaired by their caring responsibilities. Indeed, both young and adult carers alike had few opportunities to develop friendships or social contacts, or indeed to act on their ambitions and personal interests (which could open up new avenues of experience to them) because of the pragmatics of caring, as well as the psychological impact of constantly planning for and attending to their parent/s needs. Indeed, the relentless routine of their lives negated any opportunities to savour novel experiences.

In terms of praise and recognition, our findings clearly reveal little recognition for children as unpaid informal carers in the community. No attempts were made to allay their fears and anxieties by professionals paid to care.

Indeed, although young carers were not being identified or recognised, the mechanisms for recognition do exist, for example in school. However, our findings reveal that even in school young carers remained largely unacknowledged, and when they were identified, for example, by teaching staff, their circumstances were either ignored or their caring accounts treated with scepticism and disbelief. Furthermore, young carers were sometimes humiliated through the practice of classroom confrontation - young carers were required to explain their lateness or absences to their teachers in front of their classmates.

Young carers' opportunities for praise were equally limited and the only areas where praise could be administered was once again within the confines of the caring relationship - the care receiver's grateful - loving - acknowledgements of their child/ren's continual support. Often cosmetic accolades may come from outsiders or the media, who, as Meredith (1991b:15) suggests present young carers as 'little angels'.

Clearly, the gradual extension of responsibilities among children bears little relation to the actual experience of children who care. The WHO study suggested that such responsibilities should start with very simple personal routines. Young carers' routines on the other hand were entirely selfless and often of a very demanding and intimate nature. Young carers' introduction to adulthood and caring was often unexpected and sometimes violent. Furthermore, their lack of choice in undertaking their caring roles meant that they had no opportunities to increase their autonomy through the *moderate* and measured commencement of responsibility.

The challenge to policy makers must be to 'ensure the opportunity for optimal flowering of each individual's autonomy' (Doyal and Gough, 1991:207). Young carers need to be given the recognition, opportunity and support to flower as individuals, children *and* carers.

Principles, Guidelines and Approaches for Action

In considering provision for young carers it is important that, as adults, we do not impose our own ideals concerning their best interests. Nor should we assume that models which apply to adult carers, or groups of other people in need, would work equally well for young carers.

We believe that guidelines or approaches for action should be based upon child carer's own statements of need. Indeed, the starting point when considering the way forward is to acknowledge the unique situation of each young carer; so that any assessment of their needs is made on an individual basis. What is right for one young carer might not be right for another.

A Rights Based Approach

Furthermore, any guidelines for the provision of young carers' needs or service delivery must inevitably be based on philosophical and pragmatic principles. These include the recognition and observation of children's rights, practical policy recommendations based upon these rights and pragmatic considerations in relation to professional intervention and service arrangements. Alderson (1992:156) has suggested that 're-thinking childhood in terms of rights opens the way for children to be consulted more fully in defining their interests'.

It would be inappropriate for us to list here a series of 'demands' from caring agencies and organisations. The young carers in our study have very ably articulated their own needs and what they feel they require, in terms of services and support. These are outlined in chapter six. To a large extent their expressed needs for *services* are modest.

What we want to do in the remainder of this chapter is to provide some of the general principles that might serve to guide the *development* of *specific* responses and services to children who care. The framework we suggest is based upon the understanding that children who care are both children *and* carers, and have rights as such. We wholly accept, indeed much of this report has highlighted, the tensions inherent in being a child and being a carer at the same time. Nonetheless, the young carers in our study wanted to hold on to both of these worlds. What they wanted from *others*, including paid professionals, was for their contribution to be acknowledged, recognised and valued, and for some help in the performance of daily routine chores and intimate personal tasks. No young carer was asking to be 'taken away' from the caring role, nor were they asking for their loved-one to be taken away. What they *were* asking for was someone to talk to (who would listen and understand) and for a little help now and then.

It is difficult to frame a set of guidelines or recommendations that rest comfortably between the contradictions and tensions inherent in being a child *and* a carer. A starting point, however, is to identify a set of rights that can form the bedrock from which more detailed and specific guidelines, recommendations or approaches can be developed. These rights are tantamount to a statement of principle. We believe that young carers, as children and as carers have:

- the right to self-determination and choice (to be children, carers or both);
- the right to be recognised and treated separately from the care receiver;
- the right to be heard, listened to and believed;
- the right to privacy and respect;
- the right to play, recreation and leisure;
- the right to education;
- the right to health and social care services specific to their needs;
- the right to practical help and support, including respite care;
- the right to protection from physical and psychological harm (including the right to protection from injury caused by lifting etc);
- the right to be consulted and be fully involved in discussions about decisions which affect their lives and the lives of their families;
- the right to information and advice on matters that concern them and their families

(including benefits and services, medical information etc);

• the right to access to trained individuals and agencies who can deliver information and advice with appropriate expertise, in confidence;

• the right to independent and confidential representation and advocacy, including befriending or 'buddying';

• the right to a full assessment of their needs, strengths and weaknesses, including full recognition of racial, cultural and religious needs;

• the right to appeal and complaints procedures that work;

• the right to stop caring.

Needs and Services

Moving beyond this statement of rights, to considering more specific service provision and professional interventions, requires us to consider a number of other factors and issues. However, a general 'test' for any service development or provision will be the extent to which it measures up against - indeed promotes - the set of rights identified above.

Our findings reveal that young carers' needs are neither manifold nor particularly complex. In terms of provision, a need for 'someone to talk to' should not place untold strain on resources, whichever sector these resources might come from. However, it must be acknowledged that, in future, local authority social services departments will play the key, pivotal role in assessing the needs of carers, even if they do not directly provide services or support in response. Effective training and assessment procedures will have to be established to ensure that

young carers are firstly identified and secondly assessed.

Many local authorities have still to work out their assessment procedures for carers. The 'triggers' that lead to partial or full assessments are critical to this process. We would argue that, in all households where the primary carer is a child, a full assessment of that child's needs should be an automatic response.

What is worrying, however, is that identification and assessment may, in the brave new world of community care, not necessarily lead to the provision of specific services. The division between *assessment* and *responding* to need or service provision, seems to grow increasingly wider the closer we move towards final implementation of the community care reforms in April 1993. Guidance warns authorities against 'raising expectations that cannot be met'. As far as young carers are concerned, they have few expectations, and most of these have never before been met by professionals paid to care. It would be foolhardy to predict that the future will be any better. We can only hope that it will be. But we can also provide suggestions as to how it *might* be done.

One immediate, and very real help to young carers would be the provision of adequate information and advice. At present, many young carers are not receiving the information which is crucial to their day-to-day quality of life, and which could give them the opportunity to better express their own needs in terms of services. Again, the provision of information need not be a severe burden on resources and finances. The development of 'resource and information packs' for young carers and their families could provide much of the information - on advice and counselling agencies, benefits, medical information or 'helplines' etc - that is needed.

The development of such resources, and other new services or arrangements, will need to take full account of the racial, cultural and religious needs of young carers and their families, as our statement of rights above shows. But they will also have to take account of educational ability and literacy. Some young carers cannot read or write. They will need access to information that is not in written form. Another service that would have an immediate benefit for many children who care would be the establishment of some befriending or 'buddying' scheme, for social purposes, as well as advice. We refer to this in more detail in chapter six.

What is also clear from the findings is that any services, or packages of care provided by professionals or volunteers will need to be flexible and tailored to meet the individual needs of young carers.

This will require service planners and providers to be trained, sensitive and proactive - rather than just responding to crises as they arise. But it will also require improved inter-agency and inter-professional communication. Young carers have often fallen into the gaps between social services and education, and between health and social care. Agencies need to work together *for* children who care, rather than *against* them. There are too many examples cited by young carers of one agency following a particular line (eg prosecution for non school attendance) which only serves to exacerbate

an already precarious situation. Or there are other examples where the presence of a young carer has gone wholly unrecognised, despite the family being in contact with a social worker, GP or district nurse.

Some local authorities have started to employ development workers whose brief is to identify and work with young carers in a particular locality or neighbourhood. Whilst we support these initiatives, we are concerned that many carers (adults and children) are often *not* identified by professionals, nor may they wish to be identified. It is too early to be categorical about the value, or otherwise, of such neighbourhood developments, but their advantages and disadvantages need to be weighed up when considering future responses and actions.

In this chapter we have tried to provide some general principles, based on the rights of children as carers, from which services might be provided, and also evaluated. Our concern is not to argue for one particular approach or to set out a series of 'demands'. What we want to do is provoke discussion and debate; to open up the world of young carers to a wider, perhaps more responsive and sensitive audience. The challenge for the future is to engage with these issues, to do something for children who care. As Alison and Jimmy said:

> *I agreed to take part in this research because it's important everyone knows how we feel and how we've been ignored. Something has got to be done to help young carers.*
> (Alison)

It's too late for me now. My dad died and I'm no longer a 'young carer', but for all those other kids out there who are in the same situation I was, then something should be done to help them. Not take them away from their mum or dad, but to help them care without worrying, without being frightened.

(Jimmy)

Appendix (Methodology)

Literature Review

A literature search was undertaken to identify all the available research on young carers. The relatively recent emergence of this issue onto the social policy agenda meant there had been very little academic work undertaken. However, certain texts incorporated the issue of young caring through the examination of wider issues (for example medical texts which examined the impact of certain illnesses and disabilities).

The literature review also included an historical analysis in terms of novellic images of young carers, as well as testimonial evidence in non fictional texts. Such an historical perspective was intended to illustrate that young carers are not simply a contemporary phenomenon, and that they have remained hidden and neglected in the community and in the policy making process.

Steering Group

The research was supported by a multi-disciplinary steering group made up of professionals from health, social services, education and voluntary and carers organisations in Nottinghamshire. By meeting regularly throughout the project's duration, steering group members lent their expertise and guidance.

Publicity Material

Prior to the interviews with the professionals to identify young carers, it was necessary to produce project material which would serve as publicity for the research. This was mainly used to inform professionals about the nature and aims of the study and also to reassure them about issues of confidentiality.

This material also helped inform media professionals, as appeals were broadcast on local community radio stations for young carers to participate in the research. Media involvement at this stage was kept to a minimum, but it was hoped that the community radio appeals would serve as an important exercise in assessing a) if young people would come forward on the strength of the broadcast; b) if it would facilitate access to individuals who were not known to any professionals; or c) if young people would be willing to come forward independent of intermediaries (ie their social workers, health visitors etc), which would entail self-selection and identification of themselves as young carers.

Unfortunately no young carers were identified by this method. Suggested reasons for this lack of response could be the lack of ability of young carers to identify themselves in the caring role; lack of incentive (no participatory 'reward' was offered) or fear of the consequences of participation.

Interviews with Professionals

Interviews were conducted with members of the project's steering group and other relevant professionals from health, education, social services and voluntary sectors. These interviews were intended a) to ascertain the level of awareness of the young caring issue b) to discuss the stresses and strains on children who care and identify solutions, and c) wherever possible to obtain names of young carers known to these professionals in their work.

During these interviews it was necessary to offer reassurances about supplying names, to counteract levels of suspicion and distrust among those who had encountered young carers in their work. There was an understandable prevailing tendency to protect the child (even though in many cases the child was not the client) and many concerns were expressed about ethical issues and confidentiality.

Obtaining names and addresses of known young carers was a long and difficult process. Often there was a necessary period of referral by a case worker, either to social work teams or line managers. This often took some considerable time. Some professionals agreed immediately to provide contact names; some agreed but then would not provide any background details (which meant approaching the young carer's family 'cold'). Some professionals wanted to be present during the interviews, but were successfully discouraged on the grounds that their presence might constrain the young carer and lead to confusion over the 'independence' of the research.

It became clear that the professional perspective was often at variance with that of the young carers. For example, the professional involved would anticipate the young carer's response to participating in the research. They would be negative about the young carer's willingness to be interviewed, when in fact in each case the young carers were more than willing to take part. It was necessary once again to engage in reassurances to counteract these tendencies towards over protection of the young carers.

Interviews with Young Carers

In most cases, the professionals involved obtained parental permission for an initial approach to be made to the young carer by the researcher. Or, through familiarity with a particular case, the professional had assessed the young carer's potential level of interest and willingness to participate.

In each case the researcher contacted young carers by telephone, following an initial discussion with the parents or adults in the family. At no point were the young carers or their parents approached by post because this would have allowed the young carer to respond negatively (or indeed ignore the request completely), and did not facilitate a personal approach in which reassurances could be offered and some sort of rapport established.

No parents/adults refused to give their permission for the interview to take place and none of the young carers refused to take part in discussions. The initial telephone request enabled the researcher to offer reassurances about data protection (although interestingly none of the young carers or their families expressed any concern about confidentiality).

It was a primary objective of the research to include young carers from minority ethnic communities, although previous studies had found this problematic (see Bilsborrow, 1992). Due to potential language and cultural barriers - especially considering the gender, nationality and cultural background of the interviewer - it was necessary to employ the services of a 'mediator' at the point of contact with families from minority ethnic communities.

A local Asian welfare worker, who co-ordinated an Asian women's luncheon club, agreed to participate in the research process by contacting young Asian carers known to her in her work. She proved to be a crucial intermediary and translator in those families where the parents could not speak English. All the Asian families she contacted agreed to their child/ren being interviewed, with the proviso that she was present throughout the discussions. This was considered necessary in order to gain access to Asian young carers, and her presence did not appear to effect the interview process adversely.

Although attempts were made to include young carers from African-Caribbean communities - again using appeals on local community radio - they were unsuccessful. Their inclusion would be an imperative in any future research.

The period of initial contact with the young carers was very successful, not only because it was possible to include those from minority ethnic backgrounds, but also because not one of the young carers refused to take part in the interviews.

In all, 15 respondents were interviewed twice; 11 were young carers whose ages ranged from 3 - 18, and four were adult carers who had cared since childhood (now aged between 22 - 35). Four of the young carers were from minority ethnic communities. The first interviews were conducted between July and September 1992. The second interviews were conducted in September and October 1992.

In terms of age, it was clearly not possible to conduct a comprehensive interview with the three year old (Caroline). Because of the obvious communication difficulties, many of the details of Caroline's caring tasks were obtained from her mother and grandmother, and some were observed by the researcher during the interview process itself.

The initial interviews were semi-structured, but allowed the young carers to set the tone and pace of the discussion. Secondary interviews were conducted around three months after the initial interviews. The secondary interviews also included a structured verbal questionnaire on the nature and extent of the young carer's responsibilities. This questionnaire was adapted from the National Association of Health Authorities and Trusts (NAHAT, 1991) research on definitions of health and social care.

The semi-structured interview schedule was organised in themes which included:
The caring biography - period of care; caring sequence; reasons for caring; caring routines; care receiver's profile; life outside the caring environment.
The caring period - relationship with care receiver; relationships with others; self.
Current life - financial situation; formal and informal help and support; the provision of information; effects of caring.
Preferences - who should bear responsibility of caring; services needed; who should help.
Background - other family members; housing; education; socio- economic group.

Interview Environment
The majority of interviews took place in the young carers' homes, and were conducted on a one-to-one basis. However, this was not possible in the Asian families as three out of

the four interviews included the presence of the intermediary and in each case other family members were present. Clearly this could have had a restrictive influence on the young carer's performance during interview. However in two of the Asian families the parents (who were present throughout the interview) could not speak or understand English, and their presence did not appear to affect the young carers' willingness to talk openly about their experiences.

All the interviews were taped and none of the young carers appeared to be constrained by the presence of the microphone.

Transcripts and Analysis

The tapes were transcribed immediately following the interviews and together produced 350 pages of manuscript. The transcripts were then coded thematically. Once all the tapes had been transcribed and coded they were collated and an analysis was conducted on the basis of recurring themes.

Some Methodological Issues
Gender

It must be stressed that where the interviewee was male (and a teenager) there was some noticeable embarrassment and shyness towards the interviewer (female). It took some considerable time before the male youngsters appeared to feel comfortable and began to maintain eye contact with the interviewer. Notably, these problems did not emerge where the interview subjects were female.

As the majority of the boys interviewed were Asian, the fact that the interviewee was a white English female may have been a

contributory factor. However, only one of the Asian young carers remained shy throughout the interview, and if anything his embarrassment increased as the interview progressed. This was the most problematic of all the interviews, and despite reassurances and prompts he consistently answered in monosyllables. It was quite clear that he felt uncomfortable in the interview situation, consequently the discussion was cut short (this accounts for the gaps in his biographical data - see Table 2.1).

When considering levels of embarrassment and shyness, it is important to stress that for many of the young carers the interviews represented the first time they had spoken about their caring responsibilities. With this in mind, the resulting discussions were very encouraging, as the majority of the young carers proved very willing to talk about their experiences. Indeed, following the interviews two of the respondents said they had found the discussions very therapeutic.

Status

Certain complex methodological issues arise when interviewing children. However, the young carers' unique position as children, but with adult responsibilities, complicates the issue further. Their status as children could to some extent create certain prejudices concerning their levels of understanding; but this in turn is influenced by the nature and extent of their responsibilities as carers. Biologically and in law they may be considered children, but their position as carers confers on them the duties and responsibilities usually pertaining to adulthood.

The interviews were conducted bearing these issues in mind. Furthermore, as the young carers' ages varied considerably, it was necessary to try and ascertain individual levels of understanding (usually clear from the telephone conversation and initial discussion prior to the interview, as well as through the use of 'trial' questions during the interviews) without patronising them.

Although the interviews were semi-structured, the discussions were generally based on the principle of allowing the young carers to establish the flow and tone of the conversation, with appropriate prompting and direction where necessary.

The fact that most of the young carers were talking about their caring experiences for the first time, coupled with the fact that many of them were initially somewhat wary of the consequences of their participation, meant that reassurances were imperative. It was essential that the young carers were assured their participation would not result in further professional (or voluntary) intervention in their lives. Thus, it was essential that the researcher not only verbalised such assurances, but also did not in any way appear to be associated with 'authority'. Two basic factors were involved: Trust and Vocabulary.

Trust

As many of the young carers were clearly wary of inviting professional intervention into their lives, it was essential to establish and maintain a relationship based on trust. This was achieved by employing three tactics or skills: explanation, reassurance and empathy.

It was essential that the young carers understood precisely what form the interviews would take. It was therefore necessary to explain the interview procedure to them (with the emphasis on informality), how the completed tapes would be used and what the aims of the research were. It was also essential that the young carers were effectively reassured about any concerns they may have had regarding the research and interview procedure.

Furthermore, it was essential to have empathy for the young carer's conditions and circumstances. This helped to maintain the trust relationship and also encouraged the young carers to talk more openly about their experiences. Empathising with the young carers would sometimes necessitate jeopardising neutrality. For example, we found that young carers are often suspicious and resentful of authority figures they had contact with, and sometimes it was necessary for the researcher to actually encourage these sentiments to be expressed. Thus, in empathising with the young carer, the researcher was often forced to relinquish a passive, neutral position and engage in what might be seen as 'collusion' with the young carer during discussions about professionals. It is unlikely that young carers would have expressed their concern if the researcher had attempted to maintain impartiality, and 'distance'. Qualitative research of this nature inevitably brings the researcher and subject closer together.

Another important point is that it was often necessary during the interviews to ask potentially embarrassing questions, especially concerning the performance of intimate tasks.

It was essential at this point for the interviewer not to elicit any signs of embarrassment, and maintaining eye contact was very important. This was especially applicable when dealing with young carers who had not yet adjusted to their intimate caring responsibilities, and were inhibited in talking about them.

Vocabulary

An important methodological issue was the language employed to engage the young carers in the interview process, and to encourage them to express themselves freely.

It was necessary to experiment with certain questions. For example when one young carer did not respond when asked 'does your situation depress you?', it was necessary to replace this with a less complex question ie 'does this make you sad?'.

Often it was necessary to employ mechanisms to counteract inarticulateness caused by anxiety and shyness, through the use of repetition, summary and example. The repetition and summarisation of responses was often required in order to maintain the flow of the discussion and counteract misunderstanding.

It was also sometimes necessary to supply examples, especially when the young carers did not understand a particular question or were uncertain how to answer. For example, one respondent did not answer when asked: 'what would most make you happy at this time?', thus pre-determined examples were provided: 'winning the pools, a holiday?...' All these methods were used to counteract confusion and misunderstanding, and they also helped the young carers organise their responses, especially when they were particularly confused, for example when trying to recall the caring sequence or 'bad times' in their lives.

On occasions it was necessary to inject the interviews with humour in order to relieve stress or shyness. Used discerningly, humour could often relieve a young carer's distress when talking about difficult times in their lives. In her work with HIV, AIDS and children, Hongisbaum also recognises the importance of humour in the discourse with children: 'Finally, the educators should joke, using humour judiciously, to diffuse anxiety and discomfort' (Honigsbaum, 1991:55).

Bibliography

Audit Commission, (1992), *Community Care: Managing the Cascade of Change*, HMSO.

Beardshaw, V. and Towell, D. (1990), *Assessment and Case Management - Implications for the Implementation of 'Caring for People'*, Briefing paper 10, King's Fund Institute.

Becker, S. (1993), 'Personal Social Services', in Catteral, P. (ed.) *Contemporary Britain: An Annual Review 1993*, Basil Blackwell.

Bilsborrow, S. (1992), *"You Grow Up Fast As Well..."Young Carers on Merseyside*, Carers National Association, Personal Social Services Society and Barnardos.

Blunden, R. (1992), 'Community Care in the 1990s', *KF News*, Vol 15 No.1, March, King's Fund Centre.

Braithwaite, V. A. (1992), 'Bound To Care', *Journal of Social Policy*, Vol 21, Part Two.

Brimblecombe, F. and Russell, P. (1988), *Honeylands: Developing a Service for Families with Handicapped Children*, National Children's Bureau.

Caring Costs, (1992), *Taking Care, Making Do: The Costs of Caring for a Disabled Person at Home*, Caring Costs, The Campaign for an Independent Income for Carers.

Carers National Association, (1992a), 'Time to Listen to Carers', *The Carer. The Journal of the Carers National Association*, No. 24, NCA.

Carers National Association, (1992b), *Speak Up, Speak Out*, CNA.

Charteris, S. and Wheeler, R. (1992), *Paying for Services and Social Justice - A Local Authority Perspective*, Paper for the Social Policy Association 26th Annual Conference, Nottingham University, July.

The Children's Legal Centre, (1992), 'A Children's Manifesto' *Childright*, March.

The Children's Society, Unicef UK and National Children's Bureau, (1991), *Children Now: A Review of 1991*, The Children's Society, Unicef UK and NCB.

Coleman, J. C. and Hendry, L. (1990), *The Nature of Adolescence*, (2nd Ed), Routledge.

Coote, A. (1992), *The Welfare of Citizens: Developing New Social Rights*, Institute for Public Policy Research.

Craig, G. (1991), *Cash or Care: A Question of Choice*, Social Policy Research Unit, University of York.

Crompton, M. (1990), *Attending to Children*, Edward Arnold.

Crompton, M. (1992), *Children and Counselling*, Edward Arnold.

Dickens, C. (1857), *Little Dorrit*, re-printed 1985, Penguin.

DOH/DSS, (1989), *Caring for People: Community Care in the Next Decade and Beyond*, HMSO.

Doyal, L. and Gough, I. (1991), *A Theory of Human Need*, Macmillan.

East Sussex Care for the Carers Council, (1992), *Care Management and Assessment - Carers Involvement in East Sussex*, Care for the Carers Council.

Fallon, K. (1990), 'An Involuntary Workforce' *Community Care*, 4 January.

Fenwick, J. (1992), 'Policy Research in Local Government', *Local Government Policy Making*, Vol 18, No 4, March.

Finch, J. and Groves, D. (eds.) (1983), *A Labour of Love: Women, Work and Caring* , Routledge and Kegan Paul.

Fraser, D. (1973), *The Evolution of the British Welfare State*, Anchor Press.

Furnham, A. and Gunter, B. (1989), *The Anatomy of Adolescence*, Routledge.

Furnham, A. and Gunter, B. (1991), *Young People's Understanding of Society*, Routledge.

Gardner, R. (1992), *Supporting Families: Preventive Social Work in Practice*, National Children's Bureau.

Gatiss, S. and Russell, P. (1992), *Help Starts Here, A Guide for Parents of Children with Special Needs*, National Children's Bureau.

Glendinning, C. (1990), 'Dependency and Interdependency: The Incomes of Informal Carers and the Impact of Social Security ', *Journal of Social Policy*, Vol 19.

Glendinning, C. (1992), *The Costs of Informal Care: Looking Inside the Household*, SPRU, HMSO.

Glennerster, H. (1992), *Paying for Welfare: Issues for the Nineties*, London School of Economics.

Le Grand, J. (1992), *Paying For or Providing Welfare?*, School for Advanced Urban Studies, University of Bristol.

Grewal, I., Smith, I and Berry, S. (1992), *Home and Away: Parents' Views on Respite Care in Nottinghamshire*, Performance Review and Research Unit, Nottinghamshire County Council.

Grimshaw, R. (1991), *Children of Parents with Parkinson's Disease: A Research Report for the Parkinson's Disease Society*, National Children's Bureau.

Hadley, J. (1992), *All Change for Carers? Report of One-day Conference*, King's Fund Centre.

Harding, T. (1992), *Great Expectations...and Spending on Social Services*, Policy Forum Paper No.1, January, National Institute for Social Work.

Hardy, T. (1891), *Tess of the D'Urbervilles*, re-printed 1984, Penguin.

Harper, P. (1986), 'The Prevention of Huntington's Chorea: The Milory Lecture 1985', *Journal of the Royal College of Physicians of London*, Vol. 20 No.1, January.

Henwood, M., Jowell, T. and Wistow, G. (1991), 'All Things Come (To Those Who Wait?)', *Briefing Paper 12*, King's Fund Institute.

Honigsbaum, N. (1991), *HIV, AIDS and Children: A Cause for Concern*, National Children's Bureau.

Kellmer-Pringle, M. (1980), *The Needs of Children*, (2nd Edn), Hutchinson.

King's Fund Centre, (1992a), *Carer's Needs: A 10 Point Plan for Carers*, King's Fund Centre.

King's Fund Centre, (1992b), *Young Carers in Black and Minority Ethnic Communities: Workshop Day Report*, King's Fund Centre.

Kroger, J. (1989), *Identity in Adolescence: The Balance Between Self and Other*, Routledge.

Lart, R. and Means, R. (1992), *User Empowerment and Buying Community Care: Reflections on the Emerging Debate About Charging Policies*, School for Advanced Urban Studies (draft), University of Bristol.

Lewis, J. and Meredith, B. (1988), *Daughters Who Care*, Routledge.

Lindsay, M. J. (1992), 'An Introduction to Children's Rights', *Highlight*, National Children's Bureau.

McCalman, J. (1990), *The Forgotten People: A Study of Carers in Three Minority Ethnic Communities*, King's Fund Centre.

McLaughlin, M. M. (1974), 'Survivors and Surrogates', in *The History of Childhood*, De Mause, L. (Ed), Souvenir Press.

De Mause, L. (1974), 'The Evolution of Childhood', in *The History of Childhood*, Souvenir Press.

Meredith, H. (1990), 'A New Awareness', *Community Care*, 22 February.

Meredith, H. (1991a), 'Developing Support for Young Carers', *The Carer*, January.

Meredith, H. (1991b), 'Young Carers', *Contact*, Summer.

Meredith, H. (1991c), 'Young Carers: The Unacceptable Face of Community Care', *Social Work and Social Sciences Review*, Supplement to Vol 3.

Meredith, H. (1992), 'Supporting the Young Carer', *Community Outlook*, May.

National Association of Health Authorities and Trusts (NAHAT), (1991), *Definitions of Health and Social Care. Developing an Approach. A West Midlands Study*, Care in the Community (number 5), NAHAT.

National Children's Bureau, (1992), *Children Now: A Review of 1991*, NCB, Unicef UK, The Children's Society.

NCVO Community Care Alliance of Voluntary Organisations, (1992), *Community Care Alliance Manifesto*, NCVO.

Newell, P. (1991), *The UN Convention and Children's Rights in the UK*, National Children's Bureau.

Nicholas, A. and Frankenberg, R. (1992), *Towards A*

Strategy for Palliative Care: A Needs Assessment of Nottingham Health, Department of Public Health, Nottingham Health.

Noller, P. and Callan, V. (1991), *The Adolescent in the Family*, Routledge.

North, J. (1992), *Caring for People, Nottinghamshire Community Care Plan 1992/3*, (summary), Nottinghamshire Association of Voluntary Organisations.

Nottingham Afro Caribbean Respite Care Project, (1992), *Time Out*, NACRCP.

Nottinghamshire Network for A Carer's Charter, (1990), *Charter for Carers in Nottinghamshire*, Nottinghamshire County Council.

Nottinghamshire Social Services Department, (1991), *Children In Need: Local Authority Support for Children and Families*, Nottinghamshire County Council.

Office of Population, Censuses and Surveys, (1991), *1991 Census: Nottinghamshire*, HMSO.

O'Neill, A. (1988), *Young Carers: The Tameside Research*, Tameside Metropolitan Borough Council.

Page, R. (1988), *Report on the Initial Survey Investigating the Number of Young Carers in Sandwell Secondary Schools*, Sandwell Metropolitan Borough Council.

Parker, R., Ward, H., Jackson, S., Aldgate, J. and Wedge, P. (1991), *Looking After Children: Assessing Outcomes in Child Care*, Department of Health.

Perring, C., Twigg, J. and Atkin, K. (1990), *Families Caring for People Diagnosed as Mentally Ill: The Literature Re-examined*, SPRU, HMSO.

Pilling, D. and National Children's Bureau (1990), *Escape from Disadvantage*, Falmer.

Pinchbeck, I. and Hewitt, M. (1969), *Children in English Society*, Vol 1, Routledge and Kegan Paul.

Pollock, L. (1983), *Forgotten Children*, Cambridge University Press.

Robertson, P. (1974), 'Home As a Nest: Middle Class Childhood in Nineteenth-Century Europe', in *The History of Childhood*, Souvenir Press.

Robinson, C. and Stalker, K. (1992a), *New Directions, Suggestions for Improving Take-Up in Short Term Breaks*, HMSO.

Robinson, C. and Stalker, K. (1992b), *Why Are We Waiting? Reducing Waiting Lists - Practical Guidance for Developing Short-Term Breaks*, HMSO.

Shah, R. (1992), *The Silent Minority: Children with Disabilities in Asian Families*, National Children's Bureau.

Department of Social Security, (1991), *Invalid Care Allowance: Claim Pack DS 700*, DSS.

Sinclair, I., Parker, R., Leat, D. and Williams, J. (1990), *The Kaleidoscope of Care: A Review of Research on Welfare Provision for Elderly People*, National Institute for Social Work, HMSO.

Social Services Inspectorate, (1991), *Getting it Right for Carers, Setting Up Services for Carers: A Guide for Practitioners*, Department of Health.

Stafford, D. (1992), *Children of Alcoholics: How a Parent's Drinking Can Affect Your Life*, Piatkus.

Staines, D. (1991), 'Inside the Children Act: The Dawning of a New Era', *Community Care*, 26 September.

Tester, S. (1992), *Common Knowledge: A Coordinated Approach to Information-Giving*, Centre for Policy on Ageing.

Tyler, A. (1990), 'Helping the Children to Cope', *Combat Newsletter*, Spring.

Twigg, J. (1989), 'Models of Carers: How Do Social Care Agencies Conceptualise their Relationship with Informal Carers?', *Journal of Social Policy*, Vol 18.

Twigg, J., Atkin, K. and Perring, C. (1990), *Carers and Services: A Review of Research*, Social Policy Research Unit, HMSO.

Twigg, J. (ed.) (1992), *Carers: Research and Practice*, HMSO.

Ungerson, C. (1992), *Payment for Caring - Mapping a Territory*, Paper for Social Policy Conference, Nottingham University, July.

Webb, A. (1990), 'Personal Social Services', in Catteral, P. (ed.), *Contemporary Britain: An Annual Review 1990*,

Basil Blackwell.

White, P. (1989), 'The Costs of Caring', *Young People Now*, May.

World Health Organisation, (1982), *Manuals on Child Mental Health and Psychosocial Development* , WHO.

Yarrow, L. J. (1960), 'Interviewing Children', in Mussen, R. H. (ed), *Handbook of Research Methods in Child Development*, Wiley.

children who care

~ inside the world of young carers ~

•

Jo Aldridge and Saul Becker

"When I think about all those years I cared for my dad, it makes me angry, not because I had to care for him - I *wanted* to care for him - but because I was left alone to cope with his illness for so long.

I wasn't just doing ordinary tasks like other kids might do around the house. I was having to cook for him, beg for money and food parcels so I could feed him, take him to the toilet, clean him up when he couldn't get to the toilet - because he couldn't get up the stairs towards the end.

No one should have to see their parents like that, when they lose all their bodily functions. I loved my dad and I couldn't bear to see him losing dignity - getting more ill before my eyes. But because I loved him, I wanted to be with him. I wanted to look after him. I just wish someone could have helped me and that those who interfered in our lives and made them difficult could have left us alone..."

(Jimmy, aged 16)

This is the story of young carers, children hidden from view, who provide the main 'care in the community' to their loved ones - parents and siblings - often with no help or support. It is an account of choice and responsibility turned upside down: of children having to perform the most basic, personal and intimate tasks, becoming their parent's parent; of professionals and organisations who are paid to care, but who simply look on, or look aside.

Through in-depth interviews with children in Nottingham, Jo Aldridge and Saul Becker take us inside the world of children who care. Using young carers' own words, the authors provide a critical commentary and analysis on the lost childhood of young carers, their fears and pain. But it is also about the strength and commitment that children show towards loved ones, often against all the odds. Aldridge and Becker's research, and the recommendations they make, cannot - indeed, must not - be ignored by anyone concerned to improve the position of children who care.

Department of Social Sciences
Loughborough University

Published in association with
Nottinghamshire Association of Voluntary Organisations

ISBN 0 907274 01 3

£7.99 (includes p&p)